The FBI, COINTELPRO, And Martin Luther King, Jr.

Final Report Of The Select Committee To Study Governmental Operations With Respect To Intelligence Activities

Church Committee

(US Senate Select Committee To

Study Governmental Operations With Respect To Intelligence Activities)

Red and Black Publishers, St Petersburg, Florida

First published Government Printing Office, Washington DC, 1976

Library of Congress Cataloging-in-Publication Data

United States. Congress. Senate. Select Committee to Study Governmental Operations with Respect to Intelligence Activities.
   The FBI, COINTELPRO, and Martin Luther King, Jr. : final report of the Select Committee to Study Governmental Operations with respect to Intelligence Activities / Church Committee (US Senate Select Committee To Study Governmental Operations With Respect To Intelligence Activities).
      p. cm. -- (Final report of the Select Committee to Study Governmental Operations with Respect to Intelligence Activities, United States Senate ; book 3)
   "First published by Government Printing Office, Washington DC, 1976."
   ISBN 978-1-61001-004-7
1. King, Martin Luther, Jr., 1929-1968. 2. Hoover, J. Edgar (John Edgar), 1895-1972. 3. United States. Federal Bureau of Investigation. 4. Political crimes and offenses--Investigation--United States--History--20th century. 5. Civil rights movements--United States--History--20th century. 6. Political persecution--United States--History--20th century. I. Title.
   KF31.5.G7 2011
   323.092--dc22

                                                            2011000013

Red and Black Publishers, PO Box 7542, St Petersburg, Florida, 33734

Contact us at: info@RedandBlackPublishers.com

Printed and manufactured in the United States of America

Contents

I. Introduction

From December 1963 until his death in 1968, Martin Luther King, Jr. was the target of an intensive campaign by the Federal Bureau of Investigation to "neutralize" him as an effective civil rights leader. In the words of the man in charge of the FBI's "war" against Dr. King:

"No holds were barred. We have used [similar] techniques against Soviet agents. [The same methods were] brought home against any organization against which we were targeted. We did not differentiate. This is a rough, tough business."

The FBI collected information about Dr. King's plans and activities through an extensive surveillance program, employing nearly every intelligence-gathering technique at the Bureau's disposal. Wiretaps, which were initially approved by Attorney General Robert F. Kennedy, were maintained on Dr. King's home telephone from October 1963 until mid-1965; the SCLC headquarter's telephones were covered by wiretaps for an even longer period. Phones in the homes and offices of some of

Dr. King's close advisers were also wiretapped. The FBI has acknowledged 16 occasions on which microphones were hidden in Dr. King's hotel and motel rooms in an "attempt" to obtain information about the "private activities of King and his advisers" for use to "completely discredit" them.

FBI informants in the civil rights movement and reports from field offices kept the Bureau's headquarters informed of developments in the civil rights field. The FBI's presence was so intrusive that one major figure in the civil rights movement testified that his colleagues referred to themselves as members of "the FBI's golden record club."

The FBI's formal program to discredit Dr. King with Government officials began with the distribution of a "monograph" which the FBI realized could "be regarded as a personal attack on Martin Luther King," and which was subsequently described by a Justice Department official as "a personal diatribe...a personal attack without evidentiary support."

Congressional leaders were warned "off the record" about alleged dangers posed by Reverend King. The FBI responded to Dr. King's receipt of the Nobel Peace Prize by attempting to undermine his reception by foreign heads of state and American ambassadors in the countries that be planned to visit. When Dr. King returned to the United States, steps were taken to reduce support for a huge banquet and a special "day" that were being planned in his honor.

The FBI's program to destroy Dr. King as the leader of the civil rights movement entailed attempts to discredit him with churches, universities, and the press. Steps were taken to attempt to convince the National Council of Churches, the Baptist World Alliance, and leading Protestant ministers to halt financial support of the Southern Christian Leadership Conference (SCLC), and to persuade them that "Negro leaders should completely isolate King and remove him from the role he is now occupying in civil rights activities." When the FBI learned that Dr. King intended to visit the Pope, an agent was dispatched to persuade Francis Cardinal Spellman to warn the Pope about "the likely embarrassment that may result to the Pope should he grant King an audience." The FBI sought to influence universities to withhold honorary degrees from Dr. King. Attempts were made to prevent the publication of articles favorable to Dr. King and to find "friendly" news sources that would print unfavorable articles. The FBI offered to play for reporters tape recordings allegedly made from microphone surveillance of Dr. King's hotel rooms.

The FBI mailed Dr. King a tape recording made from its microphone coverage. According to the Chief of the FBI's Domestic Intelligence Division, the tape was intended to precipitate a separation between Dr. King and his wife in the belief that the separation would reduce Dr. King's stature. The tape recording was accompanied by a note which Dr. King and his advisers interpreted as a threat to release the tape recording unless Dr. King committed suicide. The FBI also made preparations to promote someone "to assume the role of leadership of the Negro people when King has been completely discredited."

The campaign against Dr. King included attempts to destroy the Southern Christian Leadership Conference by cutting off its sources of funds. The FBI considered, and on some occasions executed, plans to cut off the support of some of the SCLC's major contributors, including religious organizations, a labor union, and donors of grants such as the Ford Foundation. One FBI field office recommended that the FBI send letters to the SCLC's donors over Dr. King's forged signature warning them that the SCLC was under investigation by the Internal Revenue Service. The IRS files on Dr. King and the SCLC were carefully scrutinized for financial irregularities. For over a year, the FBI unsuccessfully attempted to establish that Dr. King had a secret foreign bank account in which he was sequestering funds.

The FBI campaign to discredit and destroy Dr. King was marked by extreme personal vindictiveness. As early as 1962,

Director Hoover penned on an FBI memorandum, "King is no good." At the August 1963 March on Washington, Dr. King told the country of his dream that "all of God's children, black men and white men, Jews and Gentiles, Protestants and Catholics, will be able to join hands and sing in the words of the old Negro spiritual, 'Free at last, free at last. Thank God almighty, I'm free at last." The FBI's Domestic Intelligence Division described this "demagogic speech" as yet more evidence that Dr. King was "the most dangerous and effective Negro leader in the country." Shortly afterward, *Time* magazine chose Dr. King as the "Man of the Year," an honor which elicited Director Hoover's comment that "they had to dig deep in the garbage to come up with this one." Hoover wrote "astounding" across the memorandum informing him that Dr. King had been granted an audience with the Pope despite the FBI's efforts to prevent such a meeting. The depth of Director Hoover's bitterness toward Dr. King, a bitterness which he had effectively communicated to his subordinates in the FBI, was apparent from the FBI's attempts to sully Dr. King's reputation long after his death. Plans were made to "brief" congressional leaders in 1969 to prevent the passage of a "Martin Luther King Day." In 1970, Director Hoover told reporters that Dr. King was the "last one in the world who should ever have received" the Nobel Peace Prize.

The extent to which Government officials outside of the FBI must bear responsibility for the FBI's campaign to discredit Dr. King is not clear. Government officials outside of the FBI were not aware of most of the specific FBI actions to discredit Dr. King. Officials in the Justice Department and White House were aware, however, that the FBI was conducting an intelligence investigation, not a criminal investigation, of Dr. King; that the FBI had written authorization from the Attorney General to wiretap Dr. King and the SCLC offices in New York and Washington; and that the FBI reports on Dr. King contained considerable information of a political and personal nature which was "irrelevant and spurious" to the stated reasons for the investigation. Those high executive branch officials were also aware that the FBI was disseminating vicious characterizations of Dr. King within the Government; that the FBI had tape recordings embarrassing to Dr. King which it had offered to play to a White House official and to reporters; and that the FBI had offered to "leak" to reporters highly damaging accusations that some of Dr. King's advisers were communists. Although some of those officials did ask top FBI officials about these charges, they did not inquire further after receiving false denials. In light of what those officials did know about the FBI's conduct toward Dr. King, they were remiss in falling to take appropriate steps to curb the Bureau's behavior. To the extent that their neglect permitted the Bureau's activities to go on unchecked, those officials must share responsibility for what occurred. The FBI now agrees that its efforts to discredit Dr. King were unjustified. The present Deputy Associate Director (Investigation) testified:

"Mr. Adams. There were approximately twenty-five incidents of actions taken [to discredit Dr. King] ... I see no statutory basis or no basis of justification for the activity.

"The CHAIRMAN. Was Dr. King, in his advocacy of equal rights for black citizens, advocating a course of action that in the opinion of the FBI constituted a crime?

"Mr. ADAMS. No, sir.

"The CHAIRMAN. He was preaching non-violence was he not, as a method of achieving equal rights for black citizens?

"Mr. ADAMS. That's right ... Now as far as the activities which you are asking about, the discrediting, I know of no basis for that and I will not attempt to justify it."

The FBI conducted its investigation of Dr. King and the SCLC under an FBI manual provision—called COMINFIL—permitting the investigation of legitimate noncommunist organizations, suspected by the FBI of having been infiltrated by communists, to determine the extent, if any, of communist influence. The FBI's investigation was based on its concern that

Dr. King was being influenced by two persons—hereinafter referred to as Adviser A and Adviser B—that the Bureau believed were members of the Communist Party.

Officials in the Justice Department relied on the FBI's representations that both of these advisers were communists, that they were in a position to influence Dr. King, and that Adviser A in fact exercised some influence in preparing Dr. King's speeches and publications. Burke Marshall, Assistant Attorney General for Civil Rights from 1961-1965, testified that he "never had any reason to doubt [the FBI's] allegations concerning [Adviser A]." He recalled that the charges about Adviser A were "grave and serious," and said that he believed Attorney General Kennedy had permitted the investigation to proceed because:

"Stopping the investigation in light of those circumstances would have run the risk that there would have been a lot of complaints that the Bureau had been blocked for political reasons from investigating serious charges about communist infiltration in the civil rights movement."

Edwin Guthman, Press Secretary for the Justice Department from 1961 through 1964, testified that Attorney General Robert Kennedy "viewed this as a serious matter," that he did not recall "that any of us doubted that the FBI knew what it was talking about," and that although the question of whether Adviser A was influencing Dr. King was never fully answered "we accepted pretty much what the FBI reported as being accurate."

We have been unable to reach a conclusion concerning the accuracy of the FBI's charges that the two Advisers were members of the Communist Party, USA or under the control of the Party during the FBI's COMINFIL investigation. However, FBI files do contain information that Adviser A and Adviser B had been members of the Communist Party at some point prior to the opening of the COMINFIL investigation in October 1962. FBI documents provided to the Committee to support the

Bureau's claim that both men were members of the Communist Party at the time the COMINFIL investigation was opened are inconclusive. Moreover, the FBI has stated that it cannot provide the Committee with the full factual basis for its charges on the grounds that to do so would compromise informants of continuing use to the Bureau.

Without access to the factual evidence, we are unable to conclude whether either of those two Advisers was connected with the Communist Party when the "case" was opened in 1962, or at any time thereafter. We have seen no evidence establishing that either of those Advisers attempted to exploit the civil rights movement to carry out the plans of the Communist Party.

In any event, the FBI has stated that at no time did it have any evidence that Dr. King himself was a communist or connected with the Communist Party. Dr. King repeatedly criticized Marxist philosophies in his writing and speeches. The present Deputy Associate Director of the FBI's Domestic Intelligence Division, when asked by the Committee if the FBI ever concluded that Dr. King was a communist, testified, "No, sir, we did not."

The FBI's COMINFIL investigation appears to have centered almost entirely on discussions among Dr. King and his advisers about proposed civil rights activities rather than on whether those advisers were in fact agents of the Communist Party. Although the FBI conducted disruptive programs— COINTELPROs—against alleged communists whom it believed were attempting to influence civil rights organizations, the Bureau did not undertake to discredit the individual whom it considered Dr. King's most "dangerous"' adviser until more than four years after opening the COMINFIL investigation. Moreover, when a field office reported to FBI headquarters in 1964 that the Adviser was not then under the influence and control of the Communist Party, the FBI did not curtail either its investigations or discrediting program against Dr. King, and we have no indication that the Bureau informed the Justice Department of this finding. Rather than trying to discredit the alleged communists it believed were attempting to influence Dr. King, the Bureau adopted the curious tactic of trying to discredit the supposed target of Communist Party interest — Dr. King himself.

Allegations of communist influence on Dr. King's organization must not divert attention from the fact that, as the FBI now states, its activities were unjustified and improper. In light of the Bureau's remarks about Dr. King, its reactions to his criticisms, the viciousness of its campaign to destroy him, and its failure to take comparable measures against the Advisers that it believed were communists, it is highly questionable whether the FBI's stated motivation was valid. It was certainly not justification for continuing the investigation of Dr. King for over six years, or for carrying out the attempts to destroy him.

Our investigation indicates that FBI officials believed that some of Dr. King's personal conduct was improper. Part of the FBI's efforts to undermine Dr. King's reputation involved attempts to persuade Government officials that Dr. King's personal behavior would be an embarrassment to them. The Committee did not investigate Dr. King's personal life, since such a subject has no proper place in our investigation. Moreover, in order to preclude any further dissemination of information obtained during the electronic surveillances of Dr. King, the Committee requested the FBI to excise from all documents submitted to the Committee any information which was so obtained. We raise the issue of Dr. King's private life here only because it may have played a part in forming the attitudes of certain FBI and administration officials toward Dr. King.

Many documents which we examined contained allegations about the political affiliations and morality of numerous individuals. We have attempted to be sensitive to the privacy interests of those individuals, and have taken care not to advance the effort to discredit them. We have excised many of the Bureau's characterizations from the documents quoted in this report. In some cases, however, in order fully to explain the story, it was judged necessary to quote extensively from Bureau reports, even though they contain unsupported allegations. We caution the reader not to accept these allegations on their face, but rather to read them as part of a shameful chapter in the nation's history.

The reader is also reminded that we did not conduct an investigation into the assassination of Dr. King. In the course of investigating the FBI's attempts to discredit Dr. King, we came across no indication that the FBI was in any way involved in the assassination.

II. The Cominfil Investigation

In October 1962 the FBI opened its investigation of the Southern Christian Leadership Conference and of its president, Dr. Martin Luther King, Jr. The investigation was conducted under an FBI manual provision captioned "COMINFIL"—an acronym for *communist infiltration*—which authorized investigations of legitimate noncommunist organizations which the FBI believed to be influenced by communist party members in order to determine the extent of the alleged communist influence. These wide-ranging investigations were conducted with the knowledge of the Attorney General and were predicated on vague executive directives and broad statutes.

The FBI kept close watch on Dr. King and the SCLC long before opening its formal investigation. FBI Director J. Edgar Hoover reacted to the formation of the SCLC in 1957 by reminding agents in the field of the need for vigilance:

"In the absence of any indication that the Communist Party has attempted, or is attempting, to infiltrate this organization you should conduct no investigation in this matter. However, in view of the stated purpose of the organization, you should remain alert for public source information concerning it in connection with the racial situation."

In May 1962 the FBI had included Dr. King on "Section A of the Reserve Index" as a person to be rounded up and detained in the event of a "national emergency." During this same period the FBI ordered its field offices to review their files for "subversive" information about Dr. King and to submit that information to FBI headquarters in reports "suitable for dissemination."

The Bureau had apparently also been engaged in an extensive surveillance of Dr. King's civil rights activities since the late 1950s under an FBI program called "Racial Matters." This program, which was unrelated to COMINFIL, required the collection of "all pertinent information" about the "proposed or actual activities" of individuals and organizations "in the racial field." Surveillance of Dr. King's civil rights activities continued under the Racial Matters program after the COMINFIL case was opened. Indeed, the October 1962 memorandum which authorized the COMINFIL case specifically provided that "any information developed concerning the integration or racial activities of the SCLC must [also] be reported [under a] Racial Matters caption."

The first FBI allegations that the Communist Party was attempting to infiltrate the SCLC appeared in a report from the FBI to Attorney General Robert F. Kennedy, dated January 8, 1962. The report stated that one of Dr. King's advisers— hereinafter referred to as "Adviser A"—was a "member of the Communist Party, USA." Within a few months FBI reports were describing another of Dr. King's associates—hereinafter referred to as "Adviser B"—as a "member of the National Committee of the Communist Party." The allegations concerning these two individuals formed the basis for opening the COMINFIL investigation in October 1962.

It is unclear why the FBI waited nine months to open the COMINFIL investigation. The Bureau might have been hoping to acquire new information from microphone and wiretap surveillance of Adviser A's office, which was initiated in March 1962. However, it does not appear that these surveillances collected any additional information bearing on the FBI's characterization of Adviser A as a "communist."

Despite the goals and procedures outlined in the COMINFIL section of the FBI Manual, the Bureau's investigation of Dr. King did not focus on whether any of his advisers were acting under Communist Party discipline and control or were working to enable the Communist Party to influence or control the SCLC. The microphone which had been installed in Adviser A's office in March 1962 was discontinued before the COMINFIL investigation began, and, although wiretap coverage of Adviser A continued—and even intensified—the information obtained appears to have related solely to his advice to Dr. King concerning the civil rights movement and not at all to the alleged Communist Party origins of that advice. Two FBI reports prepared in succeeding years which summarize the FBI's information about Adviser A do not contain evidence substantiating his purported relationship with the Communist Party.

Without full access to the Bureau's files, the Committee cannot determine whether the FBI's decision to initiate a COMINFIL investigation was motivated solely by sincere concerns about alleged communist infiltration, or whether it was in part influenced by Director Hoover's animosity toward Dr. King. The FBI Director's sensitivity to criticism and his attitude toward Dr. King are documented in several events which occurred during the period when the FBI was considering initiating the COMINFIL investigation.

As early as February 1962, Director Hoover wrote on a memorandum that Dr. King was "no good."

In January 1962 an organization called the Southern Regional Council issued a report criticizing the Bureau's inaction during civil rights demonstrations in Albany, Georgia. An updated version of that report was released in November 1962. A section entitled "Where was the Federal Government" made the following observations about the FBI:

"There is a considerable amount of distrust among Albany Negroes for local members of the Federal Bureau of Investigation."

"With all the clear violations by local police of constitutional rights, with undisputed evidence of beatings by sheriffs and deputy sheriffs, the FBI has not made a single arrest on behalf of Negro citizens."

"The FBI has [taken] dozens of affidavits from Negro citizens complaining that their constitutional rights had been violated by city and county officials. But eight months later, there was no sign of action on these charges."

"The FBI is most effective in solving ordinary crimes, and perhaps it should stick to that."

Newspaper coverage of the report's allegations were forwarded to Bureau headquarters by the Atlantic office. Although Bureau rules required prompt investigation of allegations such as those in the Southern Regional Council's Report, no investigation was undertaken. Before even receiving the full report, Bureau officials were describing it as "slanted and biased," and were searching their files for information about the report's author.

Shortly after the Report was issued, newspapers quoted Dr. King as saying that he agreed with the Report's conclusions that the FBI had not vigorously investigated civil rights violations in Albany. Dr. King reportedly stated:

"One of the great problems we face with the FBI in the South is that the agents are white Southerners who have been influenced by the mores of the community. To maintain their status, they have to be friendly with the local police and people who are promoting segregation."

"Every time I saw FBI men in Albany, they were with the local police force."

FBI headquarters was immediately notified of Dr. King's remarks. After noting that Dr. King's comments "would appear to dovetail with information . . . indicating that King's advisors are Communist Party (CP) members and he is under the domination of the CP," Bureau officials decided to contact Dr. King in an effort to "set him straight."

The FBI's effort to contact Dr. King consisted of a telephone call to the SCLC office in Atlanta by Cartha D. DeLoach, head of the FBI's Crime Records Division, and one by the Atlanta Special Agent in Charge. Both calls were answered by secretaries who promised to ask Dr. King to return the calls. When Dr. King did not respond, DeLoach observed:

"It would appear obvious that Rev. King does not desire to be told the true facts. He obviously used deceit, lies, and treachery as propaganda to further his own causes ... I see no further need to contacting Rev. King as he obviously does not desire to be given the truth. The fact that he is a vicious liar is amply demonstrated in the fact he constantly associates with and takes instructions from [a] ... member of the Communist Party."

Two years later—in late 1964—the Director was refusing to meet with Dr. King because "I gave him that opportunity once and he ignored it."

William Sullivan, who was head of the Domestic Intelligence Division during the investigation of Dr. King, testified:

"[Director Hoover] was very upset about the criticism that King made publicly about our failure to protect the Negro in the South against violations of the Negro civil liberties, and King on a number of occasions soundly criticized the Director.... Mr. Hoover was very distraught over these criticisms and so that would figure in it.... I think behind it all was the racial bias, the dislike of Negroes, the dislike of the civil rights movement. . . . I do not think he could rise above that."

The FBI sent frequent reports about Dr. King's plans and activities to officials in both the Justice Department and the White House from the initiation of the COMINFIL investigation until Dr. King's death in 1968. Despite the fact that the investigation of Dr. King failed to produce evidence that Dr. King was a communist, or that he was being influenced to act in a way inimical to American interests, no responsible Government official ever asked the FBI to terminate the investigation. Their inaction appears to have stemmed from a belief that it was safer to permit the FBI to conduct the investigation than to stop the Bureau and run the risk of charges that the FBI was being muzzled for political reasons.

Burke Marshall testified that the "charges" made by the Bureau against Adviser A "were grave and serious." The Kennedy Administration had been outspoken in its support of Dr. King, and ordering the FBI to terminate its investigation would, in Marshall's opinion, "have run the risk" that there would have been a lot of complaints that the Bureau had been blocked for political reasons from investigating serious charges about communist infiltration in the civil rights movement.

Edwin O. Guthman, Press Chief for the Justice Department under Attorney General Kennedy, testified that Robert Kennedy viewed the charges about Adviser A: "as a serious matter and not in the interest of the country and not in the interest of the civil rights movement.... The question of whether he was influencing King and his contacts with King, that was a matter which was not fully decided, but in those days we accepted pretty much what the FBI reported as being accurate."

Guthman testified that he was told by Kennedy in 1968 that Kennedy had approved wiretap coverage of Dr. King's home and of two SCLC offices in October 1963 because "he felt that if he did not do it, Mr. Hoover would move to impede or block the passage of the Civil Rights Bill . . . and that he felt that he might as well settle the matter as to whether [Adviser A] did have the influence on King that the FBI contended. . . . " Attorney General Kennedy's reasons for approving the wiretaps are discussed at length in a subsequent chapter. Of relevance here is the support which Guthman's observations lend to Marshall's recollection that Attorney General Kennedy permitted the COMINFIL investigation to continue from concern about the truth of the FBI's charges and about the political consequences of terminating the investigation.

The Johnson Administration's willingness to permit the FBI to continue its investigation of Dr. King also appears to have involved political considerations. Bill Moyers, President Johnson's assistant, testified that sometime around the spring of 1965 President Johnson "seemed satisfied that these allegations about Martin Luther King were not founded." Yet President Johnson did not order the investigation terminated. When asked the reason, Moyers explained that President Johnson: "was very concerned that his embracing the civil rights movement and Martin Luther King personally would not backfire politically. He didn't want to have a southern racist Senator produce something that would be politically embarrassing to the President and to the civil rights movement. We had lots of conversations about that.... Johnson, as everybody knows, bordered on paranoia about his enemies or about being trapped by other people's activities over which he had no responsibility."

Intelligence reports submitted by the Bureau to the White House and the Justice Department contained considerable intelligence of potential political value to the Kennedy and Johnson Administrations. The Attorneys General were informed of meetings between Dr. King and his advisers, including the details of advice that Dr. King received, the strategies of the civil rights movement, and the attitude of civil rights leaders toward the Administrations and their policies. The implications of this inside knowledge were graphically described by one of Dr. King's legal advisers, Harry Wachtel:

"The easiest example I can give is that that if I'm an attorney representing one side, negotiating and trying to achieve something, and if the Attorney on the other side had information about what my client was thinking and what we were talking about, it would become a devastatingly important impediment to our negotiation, our freedom of action."

Burke Marshall, however, described the Bureau's reports about Dr. King and the SCLC as "of no use: it was stupid information." He elaborated:

"I was in touch with Martin King all the time about all kinds of information that went way beyond what was reported by the Bureau about what he was going to do, where he was going to be, the wisdom of what he was going to do, who he was going to do it with, what the political situation was. The Southern Christian Leadership Conference and Dr. King were in some sense close associates of mine. [Information of the type included in FBI reports] was all information that I would have had anyway."

III. Concern Increases In The FBI And The Kennedy Administration Over Allegations Of Communist Influence In The Civil Rights Movement, And The FBI Intensifies The Investigation: January 1962-October 1963

Introduction and Summary

This chapter explores developments in the Martin Luther King case from the period preceding the FBI's opening of the COMINFIL investigation in October 1962 through the FBI's decision to intensify its investigation of suspected communist influence in the civil rights movement in October 1963. Particular emphasis is placed on the internal reasons for the FBI's intensification of its investigation of Dr. King and on the interplay between the Justice Department and the FBI during this period.

In summary, the evidence described in this chapter establishes that the FBI barraged the Justice Department with a stream of memoranda concerning the Communist Party's interest in the civil rights movement and Dr. King's association with two individuals, referred to in this report as Advisers A and B, who were alleged to have strong ties to the Party. In response to the Bureau's warnings, the Justice Department endeavored to convince Dr. King to sever his relations with those individuals, but met with only mixed success. Dr. King continued to turn to Adviser A for advice; Adviser B, whose association with Dr. King and allegedly with the Communist Party had been picked up by the press in late 1962, publicly announced his resignation from the SCLC in early July 1963, although he apparently continued to associate with Dr. King on an informal basis.

During hearings over the administration's proposed public accommodations bill in July 1963, critics of the bill charged that the civil rights movement, and Dr. King in particular, were influenced by Communists. Dr. King's plans for a civil rights march on Washington in August were receiving increasing publicity. On July 16, the Attorney General raised with the FBI's Justice Department liaison, Courtney Evans, the possibility of a wiretap on Dr. King and one of his legal advisers.

The following day the FBI sent an analysis of its COMINFIL information to the Justice Department. The administration decided to continue its public support of Dr. King. During the ensuing week, the President informed the press that there was no evidence that civil rights demonstrations were Communist-inspired; the Attorney General announced that the FBI had no evidence that any civil rights leaders were controlled by Communists; and the Attorney General rejected the FBI's request for authority to wiretap Dr. King.

In August 1963, the Justice Department received a report from the FBI which apparently contained allegations extremely unfavorable to Dr. King. The Attorney General told Courtney Evans that he faced impeachment if the report was "leaked," and demanded that it be resubmitted with a cover memorandum detailing the factual basis for the allegation. The memorandum submitted in response to that request contained no information concerning Dr. King that had not already been known to the Attorney General in July, but the Attorney General permitted the investigation to proceed.

In late July 1963, the FBI opened a file entitled "Communist Influence in Racial Matters," and closely monitored preparations for the August 28 Civil Rights March on Washington. The FBI's Domestic Intelligence Division informed Director Hoover shortly before the March that Communist influence in the civil rights movement was negligible. The Director disagreed. The head of the Domestic Intelligence Division, William Sullivan, responded by recommending more intense FBI surveillance of the civil rights movement.

A. The Justice Department Warns Dr. King About Advisers A and B: January 1962 -- June 1963

The Kennedy administration's concern over FBI allegations that Communists were influencing the civil rights movement led the Justice Department to make several attempts to persuade Dr. King to sever his relations with Advisers A and B. In January 1962, Hoover first warned Attorney General Kennedy that Advisor A, a member of the Communist Party, U.S.A., "is allegedly a close adviser to the Reverend Martin Luther King." Shortly afterwards, Assistant Attorney General Burke Marshall of the Justice Department's Civil Rights Division told Dr. King that the Bureau claimed Adviser A was a communist and advised that they break off relations. According to an FBI memorandum, Deputy Attorney General Byron R. White also considered speaking with Dr. King about Adviser A, but decided against doing so when told by the FBI that revealing too much of the FBI's information might tip off Dr. King or Adviser A to the identity of certain FBI informants.

Dr. King gave no indication of breaking off relations with Adviser A, who was a close friend and trusted advisor. He did, however, apparently consider the adverse effects on the civil rights movement that his association with Adviser B might cause. In June 1962 the FBI intercepted a conversation in which Adviser A recommended that Dr. King informally use Adviser B as his executive assistant, noting that "as long as Adviser B did not have the title of Executive Director, there would not be as much lightning flashing around him." Dr. King was reported to have agreed, remarking that "no matter what a man was, if he could stand up now and say he is not connected, then as far as I am concerned, he is eligible to work for me."

On October 8, 1962, the FBI's Domestic Intelligence Division prepared a memorandum summarizing accounts that had previously appeared in newspapers concerning Adviser B's alleged Communist background and his association with Dr. King. The Division forwarded the memorandum to Cartha D. DeLoach, head of the Crime Records Division, the FBI's public relations arm, for "possible use by his contacts in the news media field in such Southern states as Alabama where Dr. King has announced that the next targets for integration of universities are located." DeLoach's signature and the notation, "handled, Augusta (illegible), Atlanta, 1-/19" appear on the recommendation.

The article was apparently disseminated, because an October 25, 1962, article in the Augusta *Chronicle* described Adviser B as a member of the CPUSA's National Committee who was serving as Dr. King's "Acting Executive Director." Dr. King publicly responded, on October 30, that "no person of known Communist affiliation" could serve on the staff of the SCLC and denied any knowledge that Adviser B had Communist affiliations. Dr. King also announced Adviser B's temporary resignation from the SCLC pending an SCLC investigation of the allegations.

A stream of memoranda from the FBI, however, warned the Justice Department that Adviser B continued as an associate of

Dr. King despite his apparent resignation from the SCLC. In December, Director Hoover was cautioning the Attorney General that Adviser B continued to "represent himself as being affiliated with the New York Office of the SCLC and, during late November and early December 1962, was actively engaged in the work of this organization." A few days later, the Attorney General was informed that Advisers A and B were planning a "closeted ... critical review" with Dr. King concerning the direction of the civil rights movement. Kennedy penned on the memorandum: "Burke—this is not getting any better."

In early February 1963, Dr. King asked the Justice Department for a briefing on Adviser B's background, apparently in response to newspaper articles about Adviser B resulting from the Bureau's campaign to publicize Adviser B's relationship with Dr. King. Assistant Attorney General Marshall noted in a memorandum that he had "been in touch with the Attorney General on this matter and is anxious to have it handled as soon as possible." Sometime later in February, Marshall spoke with Dr. King about severing his association with Advisers A and B. Memoranda from Director Hoover to the Justice Department during the ensuing months, however, emphasized that Dr. King was maintaining a close relationship with both men. Those memoranda to the Justice Department contained no new information substantiating the charges that either was a member of the Communist Party, or that either was carrying out the Party's policies.

The Attorney General's concern over Dr. King's association with the two advisers continued. A memorandum by Hoover states that on June 17, 1963:

"The Attorney General called and advised he would like to have Assistant Attorney General Burke Marshall talk to Martin Luther King and tell Dr. King he has to get rid of [Advisers A and B], that he should not have any contact with them directly or indirectly.

"I pointed out that if Dr. King continues this association, he is going to hurt his own cause as there are more and more Communists trying to take advantage of [the] movement and bigots down South who are against integration are beginning to charge Dr. King is tied in with Communists. I stated I thought Marshall could very definitely say this association is rather widely known and, with things crystallizing for them now, nothing could be worse than for Dr. King to be associated with it."

Marshall subsequently spoke with Dr. King about Advisers A and B. In a follow-up memorandum written several months later Marshall stated:

"I brought the matter to the attention of Dr. King very explicitly in my office on the morning of June 22 prior to a scheduled meeting which Dr. King had with the President. This was done at the direction of the Attorney General, and the President separately [and] strongly urged Dr. King that there should be no further connection between Adviser B and the Southern Christian Leadership Conference. Dr. King stated that the connection would be ended."

Dr. King later told one of his associates that the President had told him "there was an attempt (by the FBI) to smear the movement on the basis of Communist influence. The President also said, 'I assume you know you're under very close surveillance.'"

Marshall's and the President's warnings did not go unheeded. On July 3, 1963, Dr. King sent the Attorney General a copy of a letter to Adviser B bearing that date. In that letter, Dr. King stated that an investigation by the SCLC had proven the charges concerning Adviser B's association with the Communist Party groundless, but that his permanent resignation was necessary because "the situation in our country is such that ... any allusion to the left brings forth an emotional response which would seem to indicate that SCLC and the Southern Freedom Movement are Communist inspired."

B. Allegations About Dr. King During Hearings on the Public Accommodations Bill and the Administration's Response: July 1963

Allegations of Communist influence in the civil rights movement were widely publicized in the summer of 1963 by opponents of the administration's proposed public accommodations bill. On July 12, 1963, Governor Ross E. Barnett of Mississippi testified before the Senate Commerce Committee that civil rights legislation was "a part of the world Communist conspiracy to divide and conquer our country from within." Barnett displayed a photograph entitled "Martin Luther King at Communist Training School" taken by an informant for the Georgia Commission of Education, which showed Dr. King at a 1957 Labor Day Weekend seminar at the Highland Folk School in Monteagle, Tennessee with three individuals whom he alleged were communists. When Senator Mike Monroney challenged the accuracy of this characterization, Barnett stated that he had not checked the allegations with the FBI and suggested that the Commerce Committee do so. The FBI subsequently concluded that the charges were false.

Later that day, Senator Monroney asked Director Hoover for his views on whether Dr. King and the leaders of other civil rights organizations had Communist affiliations. Senator Warren G. Magnuson also asked Hoover about the authenticity of the photograph, the status of the Georgia Commission on Education, and the nature of the Highlander Folk School. Director Hoover forwarded these requests and similar inquiries from other Senators to the Justice Department with a memorandum summarizing the COMINFIL information about SCL:

"In substance, the Communist Party, USA, is not able to assume a role of leadership in the racial unrest at this time. However, the Party is attempting to exploit the current racial situation through propaganda and participation in demonstrations and other activities whenever possible. Through these tactics, the Party hopes ultimately to progress from its current supporting role to a position of active leadership."

In the same memorandum, Director Hoover brought up the subject of Advisers A and B's alleged Communist affiliations. He claimed that the Communist Party had pinned its hopes on Adviser A, and that although Adviser B had resigned from the SCLC, he continued to associate with Dr. King.

On July 15, Governor George C. Wallace of Alabama testified before the Senate Commerce Committee in opposition to the Civil Rights bill, berating officials for "fawning and pawing over such people as Martin Luther King and his pro-Communist friends and associates." Wallace referred to the picture displayed by Governor Barnett three days before and added:

"Recently Martin Luther King publicly professed to have fired a known Communist, [Adviser B], who had been on his payroll. But as discovered by a member of the US Congress, the public profession was a lie, and Adviser B had remained on King's payroll."

On July 17, the President announced at a news conference:

"We have no evidence that any of the leaders of the civil rights movement in the United States are Communists. We have no evidence that the demonstrations are Communist-inspired. There may be occasions when a Communist takes part in a demonstration. We can't prevent that. But I think it is a convenient scapegoat to suggest that all of the difficulties are Communist and that if the Communist movement would only disappear that we would end this."

On July 23, Robert Kennedy sent to the Commerce Committee the Justice Department's response to the queries of Senators Monroney and Magnuson:

"Based on all available evidence from the FBI and other sources, we have no evidence that any of the top leaders of the major civil rights groups are Communists, or Communist controlled. This is true as to Dr. Martin Luther King, Jr., about whom particular accusations were made, as well as other leaders.

"It is natural and inevitable that Communists have made efforts to infiltrate the civil rights groups and to exploit the current racial situation. In view of the real injustices that exist and the resentment against them, these efforts have been remarkably unsuccessful."

Burke Marshall, who aided in formulating these responses for the Justice Department, told the Committee that rumors of communist infiltration in the civil rights movement had caused the Administration considerable concern:

"At that point, in some sense the business was a political problem, not from the point of view of the support that the civil rights movement was giving the administration or anything like that, but how to be honest with the Senators with this problem facing us and at the same time not to give ammunition to people who for substantive reasons were opposed to civil rights legislation."

"Generally, for years the civil rights movement in the South and to some extent in some quarters in the North ... were constantly referred to as communist infiltrated, communist inspired, radical movements ... So that the political problem that I would identify with this whole situation would be that and not a question of whether or not there was support given the Administration by civil rights groups in the South."

C. The Attorney General Considers a Wiretap of Dr. King and Rejects the Idea: July 1963

On July 16, 1963, the day after Governor Wallace's charges that Dr. King was dominated by Communists and the day before the President's denial of Communist influence in the civil rights movement, the Attorney General raised with Courtney Evans the possibility of wiretap coverage of Dr. King. According to Evans' memorandum about this meeting:

"The AG was contacted at his request late this afternoon. He said that ... a New York attorney who has had close association with Martin Luther King, and with [Adviser A] had been to see Burke Marshall about the racial situation. According to the AG, [the attorney] had indicated he had some reservations about talking with [Adviser A] on the phone. Marshall thought he might have been referring to a possible phone tap, and passed it off by telling [the New York attorney] this was something he would have to take up with [Adviser A.]

"The purpose of the AG's contact was that this brought to his attention the possibility of effecting technical coverage on both [the New York attorney] and Martin Luther King. I told the AG that I was not at all acquainted with [the New York attorney], but that, in so far as Dr. King was concerned, it was obvious from the reports that he was in a travel status practically all the time, and it was, therefore, doubtful that a technical surveillance on his office or home would be very productive. I also raised the question as to the repercussions if it should ever become known that such a surveillance had been put on Dr. King.

"The AG said this did not concern him at all, that in view of the possible Communist influence in the racial situation, he thought it advisable to have as complete coverage as possible. I told him, under the circumstances, that we would check into the matter to see if coverage was feasible, and, if so, would submit an appropriate recommendation to him."

Reports from the FBI offices indicated that wiretaps were feasible, and Director Hoover requested the Attorney General to approve wiretaps on phones in Dr. King's home, SCLC offices, and the New York attorney's home and law office.

On July 24, the day after his letter to the Commerce Committee exonerating Dr. King, the Attorney General informed Evans that he had decided against technical surveillance of Dr. King but had approved surveillance of the New York Attorney:

"The Attorney General informed me today that he had been considering the request he made on July 16, 1963, for a technical surveillance on Martin Luther King at his home and office and was now of the opinion that those would be ill-advised.

"At the time the Attorney General initially asked for such a surveillance, he was told there was considerable doubt that the productivity of such surveillance would be worth the risk because King travels most of the time and that there might be serious repercussions should it ever become known the Government had instituted this coverage. These were the very thoughts that the Attorney General expressed today in withdrawing his request.

"With reference to the other technical surveillance requested at the same time, namely, the one on [the New York attorney], the Attorney General felt this was in a different category and we should go forward with this coverage. It is noted that this was previously approved in writing by the Attorney General.

"... We will take no further action to effect technical coverage on Martin Luther King, either at his home or at his office at the Southern Christian Leadership Conference, in the absence of a further request from the Attorney General."

In June 1969, Director Hoover told a reporter for the Washington *Evening Star* that Attorney General Kennedy had "requested that the telephones of Dr. King be covered by electronic devices and was persuaded by our people not to do it in view of the possible repercussions," and because Dr. King's constant traveling made a wiretap impractical. When the Committee asked Courtney Evans whether the idea of installing a wiretap originated with the Attorney General, he testified:

"No, this is not clear in my mind at all. The record that has been exhibited to me really doesn't establish this definitely, although that inference can be drawn from some of the memoranda. But it is my recollection, without the benefit of any specifics, that there was much more to it than this. And I have the feeling that there were pressures existing in time to develop more specific information that may have had a bearing here.

"Q. Pressures emanating from where and upon whom?

"A. I think from both sides, the Bureau wanted to get more specific information, and the Department wanted resolved the rather indefinite information that had been received indicating the possibility of Communist influence on the Dr. King movement."

D. The Attorney General Voices Concern Over Continuing FBI Reports About King: July-August 1963

Following the appearance of an article on July 25, 1963, in the Atlanta *Constitution*, titled "One-time Communist Organizer Heads Rev. King's Office in N.Y.," Dr. King announced that an SCLC investigation of Adviser B indicated that he had "no present connection with the CP nor any sympathy with its philosophy." Dr. King explained that Adviser B had been on the SCLC staff on a temporary basis since his resignation in December 1962, but that he had left the SCLC on June 26, 1963, by "mutual agreement" because of concern that his affiliation with the integration movement would be used against it by "segregationists and race baiters."

The Justice Department, however, continued to receive reports from the FBI that Dr. King was continuing his association with Advisers A and B. Shortly after Attorney General Kennedy's July 23 response to the Commerce Committee, Courtney Evans:

"Advisor B, [deleted] pointed out to Marshall the undesirability of making the specific comments ... as to giving complete clearance to Martin Luther King as Marshall had had the full details as to King's association with [Adviser A] and [Adviser B.]

"Marshall said that he was most appreciative of our warning him about these pitfalls and he would be guided accordingly in any future statements. He added that he would also appreciate our continuing to highlight for him any information concerning communist activity in the Negro movement."

On July 29, Director Hoover sent the Justice Department a report from the New York Office entitled "Martin Luther King, Jr.: Affiliation with the Communist Movement." The entry under the caption, "Evidence of Communist Party Sympathies," has been deleted by the FBI from copies of the report given to the Committee on the grounds that it might compromise informants. It was a general characterization and ran for only one and one-half lines. A memorandum from Courtney Evans described Attorney General Kennedy's reaction:

"The Attorney General stated that if this report got up to the Hill at this time, he would be impeached. He noted if this report got out, it would be alleged the FBI said King was [excised by the FBI]."

The Attorney General went on to say that the report had been reviewed in detail by Assistant Attorney General Burke Marshall who had told him there wasn't anything new here concerning King's alleged communist sympathies but that it was the timing of the report and its possible misuse that concerned him. The Attorney General went on to say that he didn't feel he could fully trust everyone in the Internal Security Division of the Department:

"I pointed out to the Attorney General that first of all this report was classified secret and was just a summary report to bring our files and that of the Department's up to date. He said that while this was undoubtedly true, the submission of the report at this time in this form presented definite hazards. He therefore asked that the report be resubmitted to him with a cover memorandum setting forth the exact evidence available to support the statement that King has been described [excised by the FBI]."

The reason for Attorney General Kennedy's reaction is unclear. It may be that he feared a "leak" of the FBI's allegations concerning communist influence over Dr. King would be particularly embarrassing in light of the Administration's recent statements in support of Dr. King. The Attorney General's insistence on a supplemental memorandum detailing the underlying evidence, coupled with the tone of the memorandum, also suggests that he was anxious to get to the bottom of the charges.

Hoover resubmitted the report with a cover letter stating in part:

"In this connection, your attention is invited to my letter of February 14, 1962, in captioned matter and to my letter of July 17, 1963, captioned 'Request from Senator Monroney Concerning Current Racial Agitation,' both of which contain information to the effect that Adviser A has characterized King [deleted by FBI]."

The relevant portions of the February 14, 1962, memorandum and the July 17, 1963, memorandum have been deleted from copies supplied to the Committee. It is clear, however, that the Attorney General had been aware of whatever information those memoranda contained when he had decided not to approve the King wiretaps the previous month.

Despite the FBI's failure to produce any new evidence to substantiate its apparently unfavorable characterization of Dr. King, the question of whether Advisers A and B continued to influence Dr. King remained a matter of concern to the Justice Department. On August 20, 1963, Evans reported:

"Today the Attorney General asked if we would continue to keep him closely informed of information received relative to Adviser B's contact with Martin Luther King. He had specific reference to our letter of August 2, 1963.

"It appears that the Attorney General is receiving conflicting advice within the Department proper as to whether there is sufficient evidence of a continuing contact between King and Adviser B to justify some action. The Civil Rights Division has expressed the thought that nothing need be done by the Department. On the other hand, Andrew Oehmann, the Attorney General's Executive Assistant, has counseled him that in his judgment there is ample evidence there is a continuing relationship which Martin Luther King is trying to conceal."

E. The FBI Intensifies Its Investigation of Alleged Communist Influence in the Civil Rights Movement: July-September 1963

On July 18, 1963, in response to intelligence reports that the Communist Party was encouraging its members to participate actively in the forthcoming March on Washington, the FBI opened a file captioned "Communist Influence in Racial Matters." Field offices were advised: "it is reasonable to assume that the future will witness a strong effort on the part of the CPUSA to inject itself into and to exploit the struggle for equal rights for Negroes. Therefore, during the investigation of the CPUSA, each recipient office should be extremely alert to data indicating interest, plans, or actual involvement of the Party in the current Negro movement. This matter should be given close attention and the Bureau kept currently advised."

The results of voluminous reports from field offices around the country concerning the plans of the Communist Party and "other subversive groups" were summarized by the Domestic Intelligence Division in a report dated August 22, 1963. That report concluded that there was no evidence that the March "was actually initiated by or is controlled by the CP," although the Party had publicly endorsed the March and had urged members to "clandestinely participate" in order to "foster the illusion that the CP is a humanitarian group acting in the interest of the Negro." The Party's tactics were summarized:

"CP leaders have stressed the fact that the March is not the be all and end all in itself. Events which subsequently flow from the March will be of utmost importance, such as following up in contacts now being made by CP members working in support of the demonstration. Utilizing the March, the Party has three basic general objectives:

"(1) Participation by CP members through legitimate organizations.

"(2) Attempt to get the Party line into the hands of sympathizers and supporters of the March through distribution of *The Worker* and Party pamphlets.

"(3) Utilize the March as a steppingstone for future Party activity through contacts now being made by Party members involved in the March."

The next day the Domestic Intelligence Division submitted to the Director a 67-page Brief detailing the CPUSA's efforts to exploit the American Negro, and finding virtually no successes in these efforts. A synopsis observed:

"(1) 'The 19 million Negroes in the United States today constitute the largest and most important racial target of the Communist Party, USA. Since 1919, communist leaders have devised countless tactics and programs designed to penetrate and control Negro population.' The 'colossal efforts' focused around 'equal opportunity,' and efforts were, presently being made with 'limited degrees of success' to infiltrate legitimate Negro organizations. '[T]here is no known substantial implementation of Communist Party aims and policies among Negroes in the labor field.'

"(2) 'While not the instigator and presently unable to direct or control the coming Negro August 28 March on Washington, D.C., communist officials are planning to do all possible to advance communist aims in a supporting role.'

"(3) 'Despite tremendous sums of money and time spent by the Communist Party, USA, on the American Negro during the past 44 years, the Party has failed to reach its goal with the Negroes.'

"(4) 'There has been an obvious failure of the Communist Party of the United States to appreciably infiltrate, influence, or control large numbers of American Negroes in this country ... The Communist Party in the next few years may fail dismally with the American Negro as it has in the past. On the other hand, it may make prodigious strides and great success with the American Negroes, to the serious detriment of our national security. Time alone will tell.' "

William Sullivan, who then headed the Domestic Intelligence Division of the FBI, testified that this "Brief" precipitated a dispute between Director Hoover and the Domestic Intelligence Division over the extent of communist influence in the civil rights movement, and that the resulting "intensification" was part of an attempt by the Intelligence Division to regain Hoover's approval. The documentary evidence bearing on the internal FBI dispute is set forth below, with Sullivan's explanation of what occurred. Sullivan's comments, however, should be considered in light of the intense personal feud that subsequently developed between Sullivan and Director Hoover, and which ultimately led to Sullivan's dismissal from the Bureau. While Sullivan testified that the intensified investigation of the SCLC was the product of Director Hoover's prodding the Domestic Intelligence Division to conform its evidence to his preconceptions, the documentary evidence may also be read as indicating that the Domestic Intelligence Division was manipulating the Director in a subtle bureaucratic battle to gain approval for expanded programs.

Sullivan testified that a careful review of the files in preparation for writing the "Brief" revealed no evidence of "marked or substantial" Communist infiltration of the movement, and that he had instructed his assistant to "state the facts just as they are" and "then let the storm break." Sullivan said he had known that Hoover would be displeased with his conclusions because Hoover was convinced the civil rights movement was strongly influenced by communists. Sullivan's prediction was borne out by Hoover's observations, scrawled across the bottom of the memorandum:

"This memo reminds me vividly of those I received when Castro took over Cuba. You contended then that Castro and his cohorts were not communists and not influenced by communists. Time alone proved you wrong. I for one can't ignore the memos . . . re King, Advisers A and B . . . et al. as having only an infinitesimal effect on the efforts to exploit the American Negro by the Communists."

Sullivan recalled:

"This [memorandum] set me at odds with Hoover . . . A few months went by before he would speak to me. Everything was conducted by exchange of written communications. It was evident that we had to change our ways or we would all be out on the street."

The Director penned sarcastic notes on subsequent memoranda from the Domestic Intelligence Division. In the margin of a report that over 100 Communist Party members were planning to participate in the March on Washington, the Director wrote, "just infinitesimal!" A preliminary report on possible communist influence on the March noted that Party functionaries were pleased with the March, believed it would impress Congress, and that a "rally of similar proportions on the subject of automation could advance the cause of socialism in the United States." Director Hoover remarked, "I assume CP functionary claims are all frivolous." Sullivan testified: "the men and I discussed how to get out of trouble. To be in trouble with Mr. Hoover was a serious matter. These men were trying to buy homes, mortgages on homes, children in school. They lived in fear of getting transferred, losing money on their homes, as they usually did. In those days the market was not soaring, and children in school, so they wanted another memorandum written to get us out of this trouble we were in. I said I would write the memorandum this time. The onus always falls on the person who writes a memorandum."

On August 30, Sullivan wrote his apologetic reply:

"The Director is correct. We were completely wrong about believing the evidence was not sufficient to determine some years ago that Fidel Castro was not a communist or under communist influence. On investigating and writing about communism and the American Negro, we had better remember this and profit by the lesson it should teach us. . . . Personally, I believe in the light of King's powerful demagogic speech yesterday he stands head and shoulders over all other Negro leaders put together when it comes to influencing great masses of Negroes. We must mark him now, if we have not done so before, as the most dangerous Negro of the future in this Nation from the standpoint of communism, the Negro and national security.

"[I]t may be unrealistic to limit ourselves as we have been doing to legalistic proofs or definitely conclusive evidence that would stand up in testimony in court or before Congressional Committees that the Communist Party, USA, does wield substantial influence over Negroes which one day could become decisive. ...

"We regret greatly that the memorandum did not measure up to what the Director has a right to expect from our analysis."

Sullivan testified concerning this memorandum:

"Here again we had to engage in a lot of nonsense which we ourselves really did not believe in. We either had to do that or we would be finished."

The memorandum stated that "The history of the Communist Party, U.S.A., is replete with its attempts to exploit, influence and recruit the Negro." After reading this entry, Sullivan testified:

"These are words that are very significant to me because I know what they mean. We build this thing ... and say all this is a clear indication that the Party's favorite target is the Negro today. When you analyze it, what does it mean? How often has it been able to hit the target? . . . We did not discuss that because we would have to say they did not hit the target, hardly at all."

In an apparent further effort to please the Director, Sullivan recommended, on September 16, 1963, "increased coverage of communist influence on the Negro." His memorandum noted that "all indications" pointed toward increasing "attempts" by the Party to exploit racial unrest. The field was to "intensify" coverage of communist influence on Negroes by giving "fullest consideration to the use of all possible investigative techniques."

"Further, we are stressing the urgent need for imaginative and aggressive tactics to be utilized through our Counterintelligence Program—these designed to attempt to neutralize or disrupt the Party's activities in the Negro field."

Hoover rejected this proposal with the remarks:

"No. I can't understand how you can so agilely switch your thinking and evaluation. Just a few weeks ago you contended that the Communist influence in the racial movement was ineffective and infinitesimal. This notwithstanding many memos of specific instances of infiltration. Now you want to load the Field down with more coverage in spite of your recent memo depreciating C.P. influence in racial movement. I don't intend to waste time and money until you can make up your minds what the situation really is."

Sullivan testified that he had interpreted Hoover's note to mean that the Director was: "egging us on, to come back and say, 'Mr. Hoover, you are right, we are wrong. There is communist infiltration of the American Negro. We think we should go ahead and carry on an intensified program against it.' He knew when he wrote this, he knew precisely what kind of reply he was going to get."

Sullivan responded in a memorandum to the Deputy Associate Director, Alan Belmont:

"On returning from a few days leave I have been advised of the Director's continued dissatisfaction with the manner in which we prepared a Brief on [communist influence in racial matters] and subsequent memoranda on the same subject matter. This situation is very disturbing to those of us in the Domestic Intelligence Division and we certainly want to do everything possible to correct our shortcomings. . . . The Director indicated he would not approve our last SAC letter until there was a clarification and a meeting of minds relative to the question of the extent of communist influence over Negroes and their leaders . . . .

"As we know, facts by themselves are not too meaningful, for they are somewhat like stones tossed in a heap as contrasted to the same stones put in the form of a sound edifice. It is obvious that we did not put the proper interpretation upon the facts which we gave to the Director.

"As previously stated, we are in complete agreement with the Director that communist influence is being exerted on Martin Luther King, Jr., and that King is the strongest of the Negro leaders . . . [w]e regard Martin Luther King to be the most dangerous and effective Negro leader in the country.

"May I repeat that our failure to measure up to what the Director expected of us in the area of Communist-Negro relations is a subject of very deep concern to us in the Domestic Intelligence Division. We are disturbed by this and ought to be. I want him to know that we will do everything that is humanly possible to develop all facts nationwide relative to communist penetration and influence over Negro leaders and their organizations."

Sullivan resubmitted his proposed intensification instructions to the field. This time the Director agreed.

The intensification was put into effect by an SAC letter dated October 1, 1963, which contained the usual allusion to "efforts" and "attempts" by the Communist Party to influence the civil rights movement, but which said nothing about the absence of results:

"The history of the Communist Party, USA (CPUSA), is replete with its attempts to exploit, influence and recruit the Negro. The March on Washington, August 28, 1963, was a striking example as Party leaders early put into motion efforts to accrue gains for the CPUSA from the March. The presence at the March of around 200 Party members, ranging from several national functionaries headed by CPUSA General Secretary Gus Hall to many rank-and-file members, is clear indication of the Party's favorite target (the Negro) today.

"All indications are that the March was not the 'end of the line' and that the Party will step up its efforts to exploit racial unrest and in every possible way claim credit for itself relating to any 'gains' achieved by the Negro. A clear-cut indication of the Party's designs is revealed in secret information obtained from a most sensitive source that the Party plans to hold a highly secretive leadership meeting in November, 1963, which will deal primarily with the Negro situation. The Party has closely guarded plans for Gus Hall to undertake a 'barnstorming' trip through key areas of the country to meet Party people and thus better prepare himself for the November meeting.

"In order for the Bureau to cope with the Party's efforts and thus fulfill our responsibilities in the security field, it is necessary that we at once intensify our coverage of communist influence on the Negro. Fullest consideration should be given to the use of all possible investigative techniques in the investigation of the CP-USA, those communist fronts through which the Party channels its influence, and the many individual Party members and dupes. There is also an urgent need for imaginative and aggressive tactics to be utilized through our Counterintelligence Program for the purpose of attempting to neutralize or disrupt the Party's activities in the Negro field. Because of the Bureau's responsibility for timely dissemination of pertinent information to the Department and other interested agencies, it is more than ever necessary that all facets of this matter receive prompt handling."

The instruction to use "all possible investigative techniques" appears to have dictated the intensification of the COMINFIL investigation of the SCLC.

This was consistent with Sullivan's assurance to Director Hoover at the end of September that "we will do everything that is humanly possible to develop all facts nationwide relative to the Communist penetration and influence over Negro leaders and their organizations."

The emphasis on "imaginative and aggressive tactics" to disrupt Communist Party activities in the Negro field appears to have involved an expansion of the COINTELPRO operation already underway against the Communist Party. In 1956, the Bureau had initiated a COINTELPRO operation against the Communist Party, USA, with the goal of "feeding and fostering" internal friction with in the Party. The program was soon expanded to include "preventing communists from seizing control of legitimate mass organizations, and ... discrediting others who [are] secretly operating inside such organizations." The October 1, 1963 "intensification" instruction emphasized this latter objective of disruption.

The intensification order appears to have been more a product of preconceptions and bureaucratic squabbles within the FBI than a response to genuine concerns based on hard evidence that communists might be influencing the civil rights movement. Because Director Hoover is deceased, the Committee was able to obtain only one side of the story. Sullivan's version depicts the Domestic Intelligence Division executing an about-face after Director Hoover rejected its conclusion that evidence did not indicate significant communist influence, reinterpreting its original data to reach conclusions the Director wanted to hear, and then basing its recommendations for action on the new "analysis." However, the memoranda could also support a contention that the Domestic Intelligence Division misled Director Hoover in order to maneuver him into supporting expanded domestic intelligence programs.

IV. Electronic Surveillance Of Dr. Martin Luther King And The Southern Christian Leadership Conference

Introduction and Summary

In October 1963, Attorney General Robert Kennedy approved an FBI request for permission to install wiretaps on phones in Dr. King's home and in the SCLC's New York and Atlanta offices to determine the extent, if any, of "communist influence in the racial situation." The FBI construed this authorization to extend to Dr. King's hotel rooms and the home of a friend. No further authorization was sought until mid-1965, after Attorney General Katzenbach required the FBI for the first time to seek renewed authorization for all existing wiretaps. The wiretaps on Dr. King's home were apparently terminated at that time by Attorney General Katzenbach; the SCLC wiretaps were terminated by Attorney General Ramsay Clark in June 1966.

In December, 1963—three months after Attorney General Kennedy approved the wiretaps—the FBI, without informing the Attorney General, planned and implemented a secret effort to discredit Dr. King and to "neutralize" him as the leader of the civil rights movement. One of the first steps in this effort involved hiding microphones in Dr. King's hotel rooms. Those microphones were installed without Attorney General Kennedy's prior authorization or subsequent notification, neither of which were required under practices then current. The FBI continued to place microphones in Dr. King's hotel rooms until November 1965. Attorney General Katzenbach was apparently notified immediately after the fact of the placement of three microphones between May and November 1965. It is not clear why the FBI stopped its microphone surveillance of Dr. King, although its decision may have been related to concern about public exposure during the Long Committee's investigation of electronic surveillance.

This chapter examines the legal basis for the wiretaps and microphones, the evidence surrounding the motives for their use, and the degree to which Justice Department and White House officials were aware of the FBI's electronic surveillance of Dr. King.

A. Legal Standards Governing the FBI's Duty to Inform the Justice Department of Wiretaps and Microphones During the Period of the Martin Luther King Investigation

The FBI's use of wiretaps and microphones to follow Dr. King's activities must be examined in light of the accepted legal standards and practices of the time. Before March 1965, the FBI followed different procedures for the authorization of wiretaps and microphones. Wiretaps required the approval of the Attorney General in advance. However, once the Attorney General had authorized the FBI to initiate wiretap coverage of a subject, the Bureau generally continued the wiretap for as long as it judged necessary. As former Attorney General Katzenbach testified:

"The custom was not to put a time limit on a tap, or any wiretap authorization. Indeed, I think the Bureau would have felt free in 1965 to put a tap on a phone authorized by Attorney General Jackson before World War II."

In "national security" cases, the FBI was free to carry out microphone surveillances without first seeking the approval of the Attorney General or informing him afterward. The Bureau apparently derived authority for its microphone practice from a 1954 memorandum sent by Attorney General Brownell to Director Hoover, stating:

"It is clear that in some instances the use of microphone surveillance is the only possible way to uncovering the activities of espionage agents, possible saboteurs, and subversive persons. In such instances I am of the opinion that the national interest requires that microphone surveillance be utilized by the Federal Bureau of Investigation. This use need not be limited to the development of evidence for prosecution. The FBI has an intelligence function in connection with internal security matters equally as important as the duty of developing evidence for presentation to the courts, and the national security requires that the FBI be able to use microphone surveillance for the proper discharge of both such functions. The Department of Justice approves the use of microphone surveillance by the FBI under these circumstances and for these purposes.... I recognize that for the FBI to fulfill its important intelligence function, considerations of internal security and the national safety are paramount and, therefore, may compel the unrestricted use of this technique in the national interest."

The Justice Department was on notice that the FBI's practice was to install microphones without first informing the Justice Department. Director Hoover told Deputy Attorney General Bryon White in May 1961: "in the internal security field we are utilizing microphone surveillances on a restricted basis even though trespass is necessary to assist in uncovering the activity of Soviet intelligence agents and Communist Party leaders.... In the interest of national safety, microphone surveillances are also utilized on a restricted basis, even though trespass is necessary, in uncovering major criminal activities."

A memorandum by Courtney Evans indicates that he discussed microphones in "organized crime cases" with the Attorney General in July 1961:

"It was pointed out to the Attorney General that we had taken action with regard to the use of microphones in [organized crime] cases and . . . we were nevertheless utilizing them in all instances where this was technically feasible and where valuable information might be expected. The strong objections to the utilization of telephone taps as contrasted to microphone surveillances was stressed. The Attorney General stated he recognized the reasons why telephone taps should be restricted to national-defense-type cases and he was pleased we had been using microphone surveillances, where these objections do not apply, wherever possible in organized crime matters."

The Justice Department later summarized this practice in a brief to the Supreme Court:

"Under Departmental practice in effect for a period of years prior to 1963, and continuing into 1965, the Director of the Federal Bureau of Investigation was given authority to approve the installation of devices such as [microphones] for intelligence (but not evidentiary) purposes when required in the interest of internal security or national safety, including organized crime, kidnappings, or matters wherein human life might be at stake."

On March 30, 1965, at the urging of Attorney General Katzenbach, the FBI adopted a uniform procedure for submitting both wiretaps and microphones to the Attorney General for his approval prior to installation. Director Hoover described the new procedures in a memorandum to the Attorney General:

"In line with your suggestion this morning, I have already set up the procedure similar to requesting of authority for phone taps to be utilized in requesting authority for the placement of microphones. In other words, I shall forward to you from time to time requests for authority to install microphones where deemed imperative for your consideration and approval or disapproval. Furthermore, I have instructed that, where you have approved either a phone tap or the installation of a microphone, you will be advised when such is discontinued if in less than six months and, if not discontinued in less than six months, that a new request be submitted by me to you for extension of the telephone tap or microphone installation."

One week later Katzenbach sent to the White House a proposed Presidential directive to all Federal agencies on electronic surveillance. This directive, formally issued by President Johnson on June 30, 1965, forbade the nonconsensual interception of telephone communications by Federal personnel, "except in connection with investigations related to the national security" and then only after obtaining the written approval of the Attorney General. The directive was less precise concerning microphone surveillance:

"Utilization of mechanical or electronic devices to overhear non-telephone conversations is an even more difficult problem, which raises substantial and unresolved questions of constitutional interpretation. I desire that each agency conducting such investigations consult with the Attorney General to ascertain whether the agency's practices are fully in accord with the law and with a decent regard for the rights of others."

B. Wiretap Surveillance of Dr. King and the SCLC: October 1963 -- June 1966

On September 6, 1963, Assistant Director William Sullivan first recommended to Director Hoover that the FBI install wiretaps on Dr. King's home and the offices of the Southern Christian Leadership Conference. Sullivan's recommendation was apparently part of an attempt to improve the Domestic

Intelligence Division's standing with the Director by convincing him that Sullivan's Division was concerned about alleged communist influence on the civil rights movement and that the Division intended, as Sullivan subsequently informed the Director, to "do everything that is humanly possible" in conducting its investigation.

Sullivan's recommendation was viewed with skepticism by the FBI leadership since Attorney General Kennedy had rejected a similar proposal two months earlier. Associate Director Clyde Tolson noted on the memorandum containing Sullivan's Proposal: "I see no point in making this recommendation to the Attorney General in view of the fact that he turned down a similar recommendation on July 22, 1963." Director Hoover scrawled below Tolson's note: "I will approve though I am dizzy over vacillation as to influence of CPUSA."

In late September 1963 the FBI conducted a survey and concluded that wiretap coverage of Dr. King's residence and of the New York SCLC office could be implemented without detection. On October 7, citing "possible communist influence in the racial situation," Hoover requested the Attorney General's permission for a wiretap "on King at his current address or at any future address to which he may move" and "on the SCLC office at the current New York address or to any other address to which it may be moved." Attorney General Kennedy signed the request on October 10 and, on October 21, also approved the FBI request for coverage of the SCLC's Atlanta office.

Two memoranda by Courtney Evans indicate that the Attorney General was uncertain about the advisability of the wiretaps. On October 10, the Attorney General summoned Evans to discuss the FBI's request for the wiretaps on Dr. King's home telephone and the New York SCLC telephones. Evans wrote:

"The Attorney General said that he recognized the importance of this coverage if substantial information is to be developed concerning the relationship between King and the communist party. He said there was no question in his mind as to the coverage in New York City but that he was worried about the security of an installation covering a residence in Atlanta, Georgia. He noted that the last thing we could afford to have would be a discovery of a wiretap on King's residence.

"I pointed out to the Attorney General the fact that a residence was involved did not necessarily mean there was any added risk because of the technical nature of the telephone system.... After this discussion the Attorney General said he felt we should go ahead with the technical coverage on King on a trial basis, and to continue it if productive results were forthcoming. He said he was certain that all Bureau representatives involved would recognize the delicacy of this particular matter and would thus be even more cautious than ever in this assignment."

According to Evans' memorandum, the Attorney General signed the authorization for the wiretap immediately after this conversation.

Another memorandum by Evans describes the Attorney General's reaction on approving the Bureau's request for a wiretap on the Atlanta SCLC office a week later:

"The Attorney General is apparently still vacillating in his position as to technical coverage.... I reminded him of our previous conversation wherein he was assured that all possible would be done to insure the security of this operation.

"The Attorney General advised that he was approving [the wiretaps] but asked that this coverage and that on King's residence be evaluated at the end of thirty days in light of the results secured so that the continuance of those surveillances could be determined at that time."

Wiretaps were installed on the SCLC's New York office on October 24, 1963, and at Dr. King's home and the SCLC's Atlanta office on November 8, 1963. The FBI made an internal evaluation of the wiretaps in December 1963 and decided on its own to extend the wiretaps for three months. Reading the Attorney General's authorization broadly, the FBI construed permission to wiretap Dr. King "at his current address or at any future address" to include hotel room phones and the phone at the home of friends with whom he temporarily stayed. The FBI installed wiretaps, without seeking further authorization, on the following occasions:

Location	Installed	Discontinued
King's Atlanta home	Nov. 8, 1963	Apr. 30, 1965
A friend's home	Aug. 14, 1964	Sept. 8, 1964
Hyatt House Motel, Los Angeles	Apr. 24, 1964	Apr. 26, 1964
Hyatt House Motel, Los Angeles	July 7, 1964	July 9, 1964
Claridge Hotel, Atlantic City	Aug. 22,1964	Aug. 27,1964
SCLC Atlanta headquarters	Nov. 8,1963	June 21,1966
SCLC New York headquarters	Oct. 24,1963	Jan. 24,1964
	July 13,1964	July 31,1964

The Committee was not able to ascertain why Attorney General Kennedy approved the FBI's request for wiretaps in October 1963 after refusing an identical request in July 1963. Burke Marshall, Kennedy's assistant in charge of civil rights affairs, testified that he could not recall ever having discussed the matter with the Attorney General. It was his opinion, however, that the decision had been influenced by events arising out of concern about possible communist influence in the civil rights movement that had been widely publicized during the hearings on the Public Accommodations Act in the summer of 1963. Marshall recalled that Dr. King had made a "commitment" to the Attorney General and to the President to "stop having any communication" with Advisers A and B. Subsequently, "information came in, not as far as Adviser B, but as far as Adviser A was concerned, that that commitment was not lived up to, and I have assumed since, although I do not remember discussing it with Robert Kennedy, that the reason that he authorized the tap ... was that he wanted to find out what was going on.

"From his point of view, Martin Luther King had made a commitment on a very important matter ... [and] King had broken that commitment. So therefore the Attorney General wanted to find out whether [Adviser A] did in fact have influence over King, what he was telling King, and so forth."

Marshall's answer to a question concerning whether anyone in the Justice Department ever considered asking the FBI to discontinue the investigation of Dr. King also sheds some light on why the Attorney General might have decided to approve the wiretaps:

"Not that I know of. [The FBI's allegations concerning Adviser A] were grave and serious, and the inquiries from the Senate and from the public, both to the President and to the Attorney General, as well as the Bureau, had to be answered and they had to be answered fully. Stopping the investigation in light of those circumstances would have run the risk that there would have been a lot of complaints that the Bureau had been blocked for political reasons from investigating serious charges about communist infiltration in the civil rights movement."

Edwin O. Guthman, the Justice Department Public Relations Chief during Robert Kennedy's tenure as Attorney General, told the Committee that he had spoken with then Senator Robert Kennedy about the wiretap when it was revealed in a Jack Anderson story in 1968. According to Guthman, Robert Kennedy told him: "he had been importuned or requested by the FBI over a period of time to wiretap the phones of Dr. King, specifically wiretap the phones, as I recollect, at the headquarters of the Southern Christian Leadership Conference and, I think, Martin Luther King's home, but I'm not certain about that.

"Robert Kennedy said that he finally agreed in the fall of 1963 to give the FBI permission to wiretap the phones, and my clear recollection on this is that his feeling was that if he did not do it, Mr. Hoover would move to impede or block the passage of the civil rights bill, which had been introduced in the summer of 1963, and that he felt that he might as well settle the matter as to whether (Adviser A) did have the influence on King that the FBI contended.... My recollection is that there had been a number of conversations with King by Burke Marshall and Robert Kennedy, and I think President Kennedy had indicated to King that he ought not to have anything to do with (Adviser A). My understanding and recollection is that King said he would, and then each time the FBI would come back and say, he's still in contact with (Adviser A) ... Robert Kennedy viewed this as a serious matter and not in the interest of the country and not in the interest of the civil rights movement, if the FBI information was accurate."

Guthman testified that he could not recall Kennedy's elaborating on the steps that he had feared Director Hoover would take against the civil rights legislation if he had not agreed to the wiretap, but gave his own opinion that "Hoover's influence on the Hill could be considerable and it could have been a form of public statement or conferring with Senators in that area."

It is also not clear why Attorney General Kennedy insisted that the wiretaps be evaluated after 30 days and then failed to complain when the FBI neglected to send him an evaluation. Evans, after reviewing his memorandum stating that the Attorney General required the FBI to evaluate the wiretaps after 30 days, testified that he assumed the Attorney General had "expected the Bureau to ... submit the results of that evaluation to him." When asked if the Attorney General had ever inquired into whether the evaluation had been made, Evans testified:

"I am reasonably certain he never asked me. I would point out, however, that the assassination of President Kennedy followed these events reasonably close in point of time, and this disrupted the operation of the Office of the Attorney General."

In March 1965 Attorney General Nicholas Katzenbach requested the FBI to submit all of its wiretaps for reauthorization. He testified:

"In late April 1965, in accordance with this program, I received a request from the Bureau to continue a tap on Dr. King's personal phone. I ordered it discontinued. It is, however, possible that a request for the continuation of a pre-existing tap on the headquarters of the Southern Christian Leadership Conference was made about the same time, and I may have approved that tap. I do not recall the date or the circumstances which would have led me to do so."

Documents provided to the Committee by the FBI reflect that in early April 1965 the Atlanta office informed headquarters that it was discontinuing the wiretap on Dr. King's home because he was moving. On April 19 the Director authorized a survey to determine if a wiretap could be placed on the phone in Dr. King's new residence with "full security." The Director's memorandum also stated that "After receipt of results of survey and Atlanta's recommendations, a memorandum will be prepared along with any necessary correspondence with the Attorney General." A memorandum from the Atlanta office the next month states: "On [May 6, 1965], Mr. Sullivan telephonically advised that the installation of this Tesur [technical surveillance] was not authorized at this time."

The Bureau has been unable to find a record of any discussions between FBI officials and Attorney Katzenbach concerning this wiretap, and there are no memoranda in the Bureau files which indicate the reason that the wiretap on Dr. King's new home was not authorized.

The FBI terminated the wiretap on the New York SCLC office in January 1964, only two months after it had been installed, "for lack of productivity." The wiretap was reinstalled in July 1964 and discontinued later that month because "the office moved." No further wiretaps were placed on the New York office.

The wiretap on the Atlanta SCLC office was reviewed by Attorney General Katzenbach on October 27, 1965, and received his approval. A Bureau memorandum recommending continuation of the coverage in April 1966 was returned with a notation by Katzenbach, dated June 20, 1966, stating: "I think this coverage should be discontinued, particularly in light of possible charges of a criminal nature against [certain SCLC employees]." Technical coverage was discontinued the following day.

Attorney General Ramsey Clark turned down two requests by the FBI for wiretaps on the phones of the SCLC, once on January 3, 1968, and again on January 17, 1969. Clark wrote the Director concerning the 1968 request:

"I am declining authorization of the requested installation of the above telephone surveillance at the present time. There has not been an adequate demonstration of a direct threat to national security."

Clark's refusal to authorize an SCLC wiretap in 1969 occurred two days before he left office, at the termination of the Johnson Administration. Less than a month later the Director informed the Atlanta office that an SCLC wiretap "is in line to be presented to the new Attorney General, and a survey, with full security assured ... is desirable." FBI files contain no indication of the disposition of this final request.

C. Microphone Surveillance of Dr. King, January 1964 -- November 1965.

From January 1964 through November 1965, the FBI installed at least 15 hidden microphones in hotel and motel rooms occupied by Martin Luther King. The FBI has told the Committee about the following microphone surveillances:

Willard Hotel, Washington, D.C. (Jan. 5, 1964).

Shroeder Hotel, Milwaukee (Jan. 27, 1964).

Hilton Hawaiian Village, Honolulu (Feb. 18, 1964).

Ambassador Hotel, Los Angeles (Feb. 20, 1964).

Hyatt House Motel, Los Angeles (Feb. 22, 1964).

Statler Hotel, Detroit (Mar. 19, 1964).

Senator Motel, Sacramento (Apr. 23, 1964).

Hyatt House Motel, Los Angeles (July 7, 1964).

Manger Hotel, Savannah, Ga. (Sept. 28, 1964).

Park Sheraton Hotel, New York (Jan. 8, 1965).

Americana Hotel, New York (Jan. 28, 1965).

Sheraton Atlantic Hotel, New York (May 12, 1965).

Astor Hotel, New York (Oct. 14, 1965).

New York Hilton Hotel, New York (Oct. 28, 1965).

Americana Hotel, New York (Nov. 29, 1965).

1. Reasons for the FBI's Microphone Surveillance of Dr. King.

The wiretaps on Dr. King's home telephone and the phones of the SCLC offices were authorized by the Attorney General for the stated purpose of determining whether suspected communists were influencing the course of the civil rights movement. FBI documents indicate that the microphone coverage, (which was initiated without the knowledge of the Attorney Generals, in conformance with practice then current), was originally designed not only to pick up information bearing on possible Communist influence over Dr. King, but also to obtain information for use in the FBI's secret effort to discredit Dr. King as the leader of the civil rights movement. By 1965, references to discrediting efforts had been dropped, and documents requesting authorization for microphones mentioned only the purpose of obtaining information about possible communist influences. The details of the Bureau's efforts to undermine Dr. King are discussed in the ensuing chapters.

The first microphones were installed about two weeks after a December 23, 1963, FBI conference at which methods of "neutralizing" Dr. King were explored. Microphone surveillance was again discussed at an all-day conference at FBI Headquarters in February 1964, attended by representatives of the FBI laboratory "preparatory to effecting coverage of the activities of Martin Luther King, Jr., and his associates in Honolulu." Justifying the need for microphone coverage, the Chief of the FBI's Internal Security Section wrote that the FBI was "attempting" to obtain information about "the [private] activities of Dr. King and his associates" so that Dr. King could be "completely discredited."

The FBI memorandum authorizing the placement of the first microphone on Dr. King—at the Willard Hotel in early January 1964—gave as a basis "the intelligence and counterintelligence possibilities which thorough coverage of Dr. King's activities might develop . . . ." The Willard Hotel "bug" yielded 19 reels of tape. A memorandum summarizing the tapes was sent to the Director with William Sullivan's recommendation that it be shown to Walter Jenkins, President Johnson's Special Assistant, "inasmuch as Dr. King is seeking an appointment with President Johnson." Cartha D. DeLoach, Assistant to the Director, showed the summary memorandum to Jenkins, and later wrote:

"I told Jenkins that the Director indicated I should leave this attachment with him if he desired to let the President personally read it. Jenkins mentioned that he was sufficiently aware of the facts that he could verbally advise the President of the matter. Jenkins was of the opinion that the FBI could perform a good service to the country if this matter could somehow be confidentially given to members of the press. I told him the Director had this in mind, however, he also believed we should obtain additional information prior to discussing it with certain friends."

The FBI was apparently encouraged by the intelligence afforded by "bugs" and by the White House's receptiveness to that type of information. A microphone was installed at the Shroeder Hotel in Milwaukee two weeks later, but was declared "unproductive" because "there were no activities of interest developed." Dr. King's visit to Honolulu in mid-February 1964 was covered by a squad of surveillance experts brought in for the occasion from San Francisco. One of these experts was described in a Bureau memorandum as the "most experienced, most ingenious, most unruffled, most competent sound man for this type of operation in the San Francisco Office;" another was chosen because he had "shown unusual ingenuity, persistence, and determination in making microphone installations;" and a third had "been absolutely fearless in these types of operations for over twelve years." More than twenty reels of tape were obtained during Dr. King's stay in Honolulu and his sojourn in Los Angeles immediately afterward. Director Hoover agreed to send a copy of a memorandum describing the contents of the tapes to Jenkins and Attorney General Kennedy in order to: "remove all doubt from the Attorney General's mind as to the type of person King is. It will probably also eliminate King from any participation in [a memorial for President Kennedy which the Attorney General was helping to arrange].

Dr. King's stay in Los Angeles in July 1964 was covered by both wiretaps and microphones in his hotel room. The wiretap was intended to gain intelligence about Dr. King's plans at the Republican National Convention. Microphone surveillance was requested to attempt to obtain information useful in the campaigns to discredit him. Sullivan's memorandum describing the coverage was sent to Hoover with a recommendation against dissemination to the White House or the Attorney General: "as in this instance it is merely repetitious and does not have nearly the impact as prior such memoranda. We are continuing to follow closely King's activities and giving consideration to every possibility for future similar coverage that will add to our record on King so that in the end he might be discredited and thus be removed from his position of great stature in the Negro community."

Hoover wrote on the memorandum, "Send to Jenkins." The summary memorandum and a cover letter were sent to Jenkins on July 17.

It should also be noted that Dr. King's activities at the Democratic National Convention in Atlantic City, New Jersey, in August 1964 were closely monitored by the FBI. Microphones were not installed on that occasion, although wiretaps were placed on Dr. King's hotel room phone. The stated justification for the wiretap was the investigation of possible communist influence and the fact that Dr. King "may indulge in a hunger fast as a means of protest." A great deal of potentially useful political information was obtained from this wiretap and disseminated to the White House.

The memorandum authorizing microphone coverage of Dr. King's room in Savannah, Georgia, during the annual SCLC conference in September and October 1964 described surveillance as necessary because it was "expected that attempts will again be made to exert influence upon the SCLC and in particular on King by communists."

The seven "bugs" in Dr. King's rooms during visits to New York from January to November 1965 were justified in contemporaneous internal FBI memoranda by anticipated meetings of Dr. King with several people whom the FBI claimed had affiliations with the Communist Party. No mention was made of the possibility of obtaining private life material in memoranda concerning these "bugs."

2. Evidence Bearing on Whether the Attorneys General Authorized or Knew About the Microphone Surveillance of Dr. King

In summary, it is clear that the FBI never requested permission for installing microphones to cover Dr. King from Attorney General Kennedy, and there is no evidence that it ever directly informed him that it was using microphones. There is some question, however, concerning whether the Attorney General ultimately realized that the FBI was using "bugs" because of the nature of the information that he was being sent.

Evidence concerning Attorney General Katzenbach's knowledge of microphone surveillance of Dr. King is contradictory. In March 1965, Katzenbach required the FBI for the first time to seek the Justice Department's approval for all microphone installations. The FBI has given the Committee documents which indicate that Katzenbach was informed shortly after the fact of three microphone installations on Dr. King, that he did not object to those installations, and that he urged the FBI to use caution in its surveillance activities. Katzenbach does not now recall having been informed about the FBI's microphone surveillance of Dr. King.

(a) Attorney General Robert F. Kennedy.—The FBI makes no claim that Attorney General Kennedy was expressly informed about the microphones placed in Dr. King's hotel rooms. The only FBI claim that Attorney General Kennedy might have been aware of the microphones is a Domestic Intelligence Division memorandum written in December 1966, which states: "concerning microphone coverage of King, Attorney General Robert F. Kennedy was furnished the pertinent information obtained, perusal of which would indicate that a microphone was the source of this information."

Next to this entry, Hoover wrote: "when?" A memorandum from the Domestic Intelligence Division a few days later explained:

"Attorney General Robert F. Kennedy was furnished an eight page 'Top Secret' memorandum . . . dated March 4, 1964. This memorandum is a summary of microphone coverage . . . in the Willard Hotel, Washington, D.C.; Hilton Hawaiian Village, Honolulu, Hawaii; Ambassador Hotel, Los Angeles, California; and the Hyatt House Hotel, Los Angeles, California. The wording of the memorandum is couched in such a manner that it is obvious that a microphone was the source."

The question of whether Attorney General Kennedy suspected that the FBI was using microphones to gather information about Dr. King must also be viewed in light of the Attorney General's express authorization of wiretaps in the King case on national security grounds, and of the FBI's practice—known to officials in the Justice Department—of installing microphones in national security cases without notifying the Department. We have examined the Bureau's claim with respect to Attorney General Kennedy's possible knowledge about the microphones and have found the following evidence.

As noted above, on January 13, 1964, William Sullivan recommended to Hoover that President Johnson's assistant, Walter Jenkins, be given a copy of a memorandum detailing information discovered through the Willard Hotel bug. Sullivan expressed doubts, however, about whether the Attorney General should be given the information:

"The attached document is classified 'Top Secret' to minimize the likelihood that this material will be read by someone who will leak it to King. However, it is possible despite its classification, the Attorney General himself may reprimand King on the basis of this material. If he does, it is not likely we will develop any more such information through the means employed. It is highly important that we do develop further information of this type in order that we may completely discredit King as the leader of the Negro people.

"Next to Sullivan's recommendation that Courtney Evans hand-deliver a copy of the memorandum to the Attorney General, Director Hoover wrote: 'No. A copy need not be given the A.G.' "

Jenkins was subsequently shown a copy of the report, but was not told the source of the information.

Shortly after the Honolulu bug, Sullivan changed his mind and recommended that the Attorney General be informed of information gathered by both the Willard and Honolulu bugs to "remove all doubt from the Attorney General's mind about the type of person King is." Sullivan suggested:

"Mr. Evans personally deliver to the Attorney General a copy of the attached 'Top Secret' memorandum. It is also believed that Mr. Evans should indicate to the Attorney General that if King was to become aware of our coverage of him it is highly probable that we will no longer be able to develop such information through the means employed to date and that we, of course, are still desirous of continuing to develop such information."

Director Hoover wrote next to this recommendation "O.K." A notation in the margin states: "Done. 3/10/64. E[vans]." The memorandum sent to the Attorney General did not state the source of the information that it contained.

When shown Sullivan's memorandum by the Committee. Courtney Evans testified that he did not recall delivering the memorandum about Dr. King to the Attorney General, but that "I assume I must have in view of this record." He doubted that he had spoken with the Attorney General about the substance of the memorandum, however, because "if I did have a conversation with him, I believe I would have written a memorandum as to that conversation." When asked if he recalled ever telling the Attorney General that the memorandum contained information obtained through microphone coverage, Evans testified:

"No, I do not. And considering the tenor of the times then, I would probably have been very circumspect and told him exactly what I was instructed to tell him and nothing more.... I think it is a matter of record that the relationship between the Attorney General and the Director had deteriorated to the point that they weren't speaking to each other. And consequently I felt that it was essential that I followed these instructions very explicitly."

A memorandum from Evans dated September 11, 1964, indicates that the Attorney General had in fact received the summary memorandum, but sheds no light on whether he was told the source of the information:

"Before leaving office, Attorney General Kennedy instructed his Executive Assistant, Harold Reis, to return to the Bureau copies of top secret memoranda submitted to him by the FBI . . . on March 4, 1964, and June 1, 1964, as Mr. Kennedy did not feel this material should go to the general Department files. These memoranda deal with activities of Martin Luther King. Reis accordingly handed these memoranda to me. They are attached."

It is uncertain whether the Attorney General understood the source of the information after reading the FBI summary memoranda. Evans told the Committee that he never received any indication that the Attorney General suspected the FBI was following Dr. King's activities with hidden microphones, and surmised that the Attorney General might have assumed the information was the product of live informants, or surveillance by local law enforcement agencies. Walter Jenkins, who also read these memoranda, told the Committee that he had not suspected that the FBI had obtained the information in them by using microphones. Bill Moyers, President Johnson's Assistant, also saw several of the memoranda concerning Dr. King, and testified that he had not realized that the FBI had collected the information through microphones. He told the Committee, however, that "the nature of the general references that were being made, I realized later, could only have come from that kind of knowledge unless there was an informer in Martin Luther King's presence a good bit of the time."

(b) Attorney General Nickolas deB. Katzenbach. — Four FBI documents appear to indicate that Attorney General Katzenbach was informed about the FBI's microphone surveillance of Dr. King. Katzenbach testified that he could not recall having been informed of the surveillance, and stated that it would have been inconsistent with his claimed disapproval of a wiretap on Dr. King's home at the same time. The Bureau's position appears in a Domestic Intelligence memorandum listing the wiretaps and microphones installed in the investigation of Dr. King:

"Attorney General Katzenbach was specifically notified of three of these microphone installations. In each of these three, instances the Attorney General was advised that a trespass was involved in the installation."

The Bureau maintains that Attorney General Katzenbach was advised of microphone placements in Dr. King's hotel rooms on the following occasions:

On May 13, 1965, the New York field office installed a microphone in Dr. King's suite at the Sheraton Atlantic Hotel in New York, pursuant to authorization from an Inspector in the Domestic Intelligence Division, apparently without Director Hoover's prior knowledge. According to a contemporaneous memorandum, the New York office had only a few hours notice of Dr. King's arrival and needed to install the microphone "immediately." A memorandum dated May 17, addressed to the Attorney General and signed by Director Hoover, stated:

"On May 12, 1965, information was obtained indicating a meeting of King and his advisors was to take place in New York on that date. Because of the importance of that meeting and the urgency of the situation, a microphone surveillance was effected on May 13."

On October 14, 1965, a microphone was installed in Dr. King's room in the Astor Hotel in New York. This installation was approved by William Sullivan, head of the Domestic Intelligence Division, again without Director Hoover's prior knowledge, "on New York's assurance that full security was available, and since time was of the essence" (Sullivan claimed that the FBI had learned of Dr. King's plan to visit New York only a few hours before.) On his memorandum informing Assistant to the Director Alan Belmont of the microphone placement, Sullivan wrote: "Memo to AG being prepared." A memorandum to the Attorney General, dated October 19 and signed by Director Hoover, stated that the Astor Hotel surveillance had been placed because of the "importance" of Dr. King's meeting with his advisers in New York "and the urgency of the situation."

On November 9, 1965, a microphone was installed in Dr. King's room in the Americana Hotel in New York. A Domestic Intelligence Division memorandum of that date states:

"On New York's assurance that full security was available and since time was of the essence [as the FBI had learned of Dr. King's planned visit to New York on that day], New York was told to go ahead with the installation.... Inasmuch as the installation will be made today (11/29/65) and deactivated immediately upon King's departure, probably 11/30/65, we will promptly submit a memorandum to the Attorney General advising when the installation was made and when it was taken off."

A memorandum to the Attorney General, dated December 1, 1965, and bearing Director Hoover's signature, stated that "a microphone surveillance was effected November 29, 1965 on King ... and was discontinued on November 30, 1965." The reason for the installation was the "importance of the meeting and the urgency of the situation."

The FBI has given the Committee copies of the three memoranda to Attorney General Katzenbach informing him that microphones had been placed on Dr. King's rooms. Each is initialed "N deB K" in the upper right hand corner. When shown these memoranda, Katzenbach testified: "Each of these bears my initials in what appears to be my handwriting in the place where I customarily initialed Bureau memoranda." He denied, however, any recollection of having received the memoranda.

The Bureau also supplied the Committee with a transmittal slip dated December 10, 1965.

"Mr. Hoover —

"Obviously these are particularly delicate surveillances and we should be very cautious in terms of the non-FBI people who may from time to time necessarily be involved in some aspect of installation.

"N deB K"

Katzenbach identified the handwritten note as his, and testified that although he recalled writing the note, he could not recall why he had written it. When asked if he recalled the "delicate surveillances" mentioned in the note, Katzenbach told the Committee:

"I don't recall, and I have nothing in my possession that has served to refresh my recollection, and nothing has been shown to me by the Committee staff that serves to refresh my recollection.

"Q. In your opinion, could this note have referred to the three mentioned electronic surveillances against Dr. King?

"Mr. KATZENBACH. On its face it says that it did . . . it would seem to me that would be a possibility. I point out that it could refer to almost anything. My opinion is obviously, since I don't recall getting the first three, that this was not associated with it, and I really don't have enough recollection of what was associated with it to say. I did see Mr. Helms on that date. Whether it related to something he asked for, I don't know."

Katzenbach added that he was: "puzzled by the fact that the handwritten note, if related to the December 1 memorandum from the Director, is written on a separate piece of paper. It was then, and is now, my consistent practice to write notes of that kind on the incoming piece of paper, provided there is room to do so."

The documentary evidence — the three notices that a microphone had been placed on a room occupied by Dr. King shortly before, and the note in Katzenbach's handwriting referring to "delicate surveillances" which the FBI states was sent to the Bureau with the last of the notices—indicates that Attorney General Katzenbach knew of the microphone surveillance but did not order it halted. Katzenbach, in denying any knowledge of the microphones, pointed to two factors mitigating against the likelihood of his having permitted the surveillance to continue once learning of it: his rejection of a wiretap on Dr. King's new home in April 1965, the fact that his handwritten note urged caution in future surveillances, and that no microphone surveillances were carried out after the date of the note.

Katzenbach's position throughout his testimony before the Committee is best summarized by a portion of a written, sworn statement that he submitted at the time of his public appearance:

"These memoranda do not indicate on their face the Bureau sought any prior authorization, or state any reasons why it was not sought. They appear to present me with information after the fact and request no authority to perform similar surveillances in the future. I believe the Bureau knew full well that I would not authorize the surveillances in question, not only because of the circumstances surrounding Dr. King, but particularly because the bugs were to be placed in a hotel room. That is among the worst possible invasions of privacy and would demand the strongest conceivable justification. Indeed, I believe this position had been made clear in written memoranda to the Bureau dating back to the 1950s, and I have a clear recollection of being critical of the Bureau for installing a bug in the bedroom of a leading member of the Mafia. I reaffirmed this position to the Bureau sometime in 1965 or 1966, but that reaffirmation may have postdated these memoranda.

"Finally, I cannot recall any memoranda at any time informing me that the Bureau had installed a tap or a bug without my prior authorization. While I authorized Mr. Hoover to do so in emergency circumstances in a memorandum written in the summer of 1965, not only does the May memorandum predate that authorization, but there is nothing in the memoranda which suggests that on any of these occasions was there an 'emergency.' Further, my calendars, which are in the possession of the Committee, indicate my general availability to the Bureau on two occasions involving these memoranda, and my total availability to the Bureau on the third. Nor do I have any recollection that the 'emergency' procedure was ever invoked by the Bureau during my term in office.

"Obviously I do not believe that I received these memoranda. Equally obvious is the fact that if I initialed them, I am mistaken in my belief."

Although apparently no microphones were placed in Dr. King's hotel rooms after the November 29, 1965 "bug" at the Americana Hotel, the Domestic Intelligence Division did make one further attempt install a microphone. A memorandum from William Sullivan to Cartha DeLoach, then Assistant to the Director, dated January 21, 1966, states that Sullivan had authorized the New York office to "bug" King's room during an anticipated three-day stay. Clyde Tolson wrote across this memorandum, "Remove this surveillance at once. 1/21," and Hoover added his "yes." Tolson added a note on the bottom of the memorandum, complaining, "No one here approved this. I have told Sullivan again not to institute a mike surveillance without the Director's approval." Hoover wrote next to this comment, "Right."

V. The FBI's Effort To Discredit Dr. Martin Luther King: 1964

Introduction and Summary

In December 1963, a meeting was convened at FBI headquarters to discuss various "avenues of approach aimed at neutralizing King as an effective Negro leader." Two weeks later, FBI agents planted the first microphones in Dr. King's hotel rooms in an "attempt" to obtain information about the private "activities of Dr. King and his associates" so that Dr. King could be "completely discredited." That same week, the head of the Domestic Intelligence Division recommended the promotion of a new "national Negro leader" who could "overshadow King and be in the position to assume the role of the leadership of the Negro people when King has been completely discredited."

The FBI's effort to discredit Dr. King and to undermine the SCLC involved plans touching on virtually every aspect of Dr. King's life. The FBI scrutinized Dr. King's tax returns, monitored his financial affairs, and even tried to establish that he had a secret foreign bank account. Religious leaders and institutions were contacted in an effort to undermine their support of him, and unfavorable material was "leaked" to the press. Bureau officials contacted members of Congress, and special "off the record" testimony was prepared for the Director's use before the House Appropriations Committee. Efforts were made to turn White House and Justice Department Officials against Dr. King by barraging them with unfavorable reports and, according to one witness, even offering to play for a White House official tape recordings that the Bureau considered embarrassing to King.

This chapter examines not only the Bureau's efforts to discredit Dr. King, but the degree to which officials in other branches of the Government were responsible for those actions. A few months before the FBI held its December 1963 conference at which its program against Dr. King was apparently formulated, the Director distributed a "monograph" about Dr. King to the heads of several Governmental agencies. Attorney General Kennedy ordered it immediately withdrawn. During the course of the following year, the FBI sent several intelligence reports bearing on Dr. King's private life to the White House and Justice Department. Although government officials outside the FBI were not aware of the extent of the FBI's efforts to discredit Dr. King, officials of the Justice Department and of the White House did know that the FBI had offered tape recordings and derogatory information about Dr. King to reporters. The Attorney General went no further than complaining to the President and accepting a Bureau official's representation that the allegations were not true. President Johnson not only failed to order the Bureau to stop, but indeed cautioned it against dealing with certain reporters who had complained of its conduct.

A. The FBI Disseminates the First King "Monograph" and Attorney General Kennedy Orders It Recalled: October 1963

On October 15, 1963, William Sullivan forwarded to Assistant Director Alan Belmont for his approval a monograph entitled "Communism and the Negro Movement—A Current

Analysis." He proposed that it be distributed to the Attorney General, the White House, CIA, State Department, Defense Department, and Defense Department intelligence agencies. Sullivan testified that the purpose of the monograph was to "discredit King."

Belmont submitted the monograph to the Director with a note stating:

"The attached analysis of Communism and the Negro movement is highly explosive. It can be regarded as a personal attack on Martin Luther King. There is no doubt it will have a heavy impact on the Attorney General and anyone else to whom we disseminate....

"The memorandum makes good reading and is based on information from reliable sources. We may well be charged, however, with expressing opinions and conclusions, particularly with reference to some of the statements about King.

"This memorandum may startle the Attorney General, particularly in view of his past association with King, and the fact that we are disseminating this outside the Department. He may resent this. Nevertheless, the memorandum is a powerful warning against Communist influence in the Negro movement, and we will be carrying out our responsibility by disseminating it to the people indicated in the attached memorandum."

The monograph was distributed on October 18, 1963. One week later, the Attorney General called Courtney Evans and stated that he had just learned that the Army had received a copy of a report about Dr. King's alleged communist activities. Evans reported to Belmont:

"He was obviously irritated. He went on to ask if the Army got copies of all reports submitted to him.... The Attorney General asked what responsibilities the Army had in relation to the communist background of Martin Luther King. I told the Attorney General ... that the Army had an interest in communist activities particularly in relation to racial matters because the military had to be called on if civil disturbances arising out of such matters went beyond the ability of civilian authorities. This explanation seemed to serve no purpose."

Director Hoover recorded in a memorandum of the same date:

"The Attorney General called and advised me there was a lot of talk at the Pentagon regarding the document.... The Attorney General anticipated that this information would leak out as the military didn't like the Negroes.

"The Attorney General felt we should get back all copies of the document. I told him ... we would get them from all agencies to which they were disseminated.... I also told him if any newspapers asked about this, no comment would be made and no mention would be made that such a document existed."

All copies were recovered by October 28.

Burke Marshall, Assistant Attorney General in charge of the Civil Rights Division under Robert Kennedy, told the Committee that the monograph was: "a personal diatribe . . . a personal attack without evidentiary support on the character, the moral character and person of Dr. Martin Luther King, and it was only peripherally related to anything substantive, like whether or not there was communist infiltration or influence on the civil rights movement.... It was a personal attack on the man and went far afield from the charges [of possible communist influence]."

Marshall recalled that he had been very "irritated" about the monograph and that the Attorney General had "thought it was outrageous." He remembered that the Attorney General had ordered the monograph withdrawn, but did not know if the Attorney General had taken any further steps to reprimand the Bureau.

B. The FBI Plans Its Campaign To Discredit Dr. King: December 23, 1963

On December 23, 1963, a nine-hour conference was held at FBI headquarters to discuss Martin Luther King. In attendance were Assistant Director Sullivan, Internal Security Section Chief Frederick Baumgardner, three other FBI headquarters officials, and two agents from the FBI's Atlanta Field Office.

A prepared list of twenty-one proposals was presented and discussed. The proposals raised the possibility of "using" ministers, "disgruntled" acquaintances, "aggressive" newsmen, "colored" agents, Dr. King's housekeeper, and even suggested using Dr. King's wife or "placing a good looking female plant in King's office." An account of the meeting written by William Sullivan emphasized that the Bureau must take a "discreet approach" in developing information about Dr. King for use "at an opportune time in a counterintelligence move to discredit him." It was generally agreed that the Bureau should make use of "all available investigative techniques coupled with meticulous, planning, boldness, and ingenuity, tempered only with good judgment," [sic] but that "discretion must not reach the point of timidity."

Sullivan's memorandum reported that the following decisions were made at the conference:

"(1) We must determine and check out all of the employees of the SCLC.

"(2) We must locate and monitor the funds of the SCLC.

"(3) We must identify and check out the sources who contribute to the SCLC.

"(4) We must continue to keep close watch on King's personal activities.

"(5) We will, at the proper time, when it can be done without embarrassment to the Bureau, expose King as an opportunist who is not a sincere person but is exploiting the racial situation for personal gain.

"(6) We will explore the possibility of utilizing additional specialized investigative techniques at the SCLC office."

Sullivan described the purpose of the meeting as:

"To explore how best to carry on our investigation to produce the desired results without embarrassment to the Bureau. Included in our discussion was a complete analysis of the avenues of approach aimed at neutralizing King as an effective Negro leader and developing evidence concerning King's continued dependence on communists for guidance and direction."

Precisely what prompted the Bureau to decide upon this drastic new approach is still unclear.

William Sullivan was asked by the Committee whether tactics such as placing female "plants" were common practices of the FBI. Sullivan testified that they were: "common practice among intelligence services all over the world. This is not an isolated phenomenon. . . . This is a common practice, rough, tough, dirty business. Whether we should be in it or not, that is for you folks to decide. We are in it .... No holds were barred. We have used that technique against Soviet agents. They have used it against us.

"Question. The same methods were brought home?

"Mr. SULLIVAN. Brought home against any organization against which we were targeted. We did not differentiate. This is a rough, tough business.

"Senator MONDALE. Would it be safe to say that the techniques we learned in fighting ... true espionage in World War II came to be used against some of our own American citizens?

"Mr. SULLIVAN. That would be a correct deduction."

Sullivan testified that the plans formulated at the December 24, 1963 meeting were in accord with "Mr. Hoover's policy." After reviewing the memoranda, Sullivan emphasized, "I want to make this clear; this is not an isolated phenomenon, that this was a practice of the Bureau down through the years. I might say it often became a real character assassination."

Sullivan was asked by the Committee whether he or any other employees of the Bureau ever objected to using these tactics. Sullivan responded:

"Not to my recollection ... I was not ready at that time to collide with him. Everybody in the Division went right along with Hoover's policy. I do not recall anybody ever raising a question. . . . never once did I hear anybody, including myself, raise the question is this course of action which we have agreed upon lawful, is it legal, is it ethical or moral? We never gave any thought to this realm of reasoning, because we were just naturally pragmatists. The one thing we were concerned about will this course of action work, will it get us what we want, will we reach the objective that we desire to reach?

"As far as legality is concerned, morals or ethics, was never raised by myself or anybody else.... I think this suggests really in government we are amoral."

On December 29, 1963, less than a week after the FBI conference, *Time* magazine chose Dr. King as the "Man of the Year," describing him as the "unchallenged voice of the Negro people ... [who] has infused the Negroes themselves with the fiber that gives their revolution its true stature." Hoover wrote across the memorandum informing him of this honor: "They had to dig deep in the garbage to come up with this one."

C. William Sullivan proposes a plan to promote a new Negro leader: January 1964

On January 6, 1964—about two weeks after the FBI's conference to plan methods of "neutralizing" Dr. King's influence and to gather information about Dr. King's personal life—the FBI installed the microphone in Dr. King's room at the Willard Hotel. As explained in the preceding chapter, additional microphones soon followed; physical and photographic surveillance was initiated; special Headquarters "briefings" were held; "dry runs" were planned; and the most sophisticated and experienced Bureau personnel were deployed to gather information that might be used in a concerted effort to destroy Dr. King's influence.

Two days after the installation of the Willard Hotel microphones, Assistant Director William Sullivan proposed that the FBI select a new "national Negro leader" as Dr. King's successor. In proposing the plan, Sullivan stated:

"It should be clear to all of us that Martin Luther King must, at some propitious point in the future, be revealed to the people of this country and to his Negro followers as being what he actually is—a fraud, demagogue and scoundrel. When the true facts concerning his activities are presented, such should be enough, if handled properly, to take him off his pedestal and to reduce him completely in influence. When this is done, and it can be and will be done, obviously much confusion will reign, particularly among the Negro people. . . . The Negroes will be left without a national leader of sufficiently compelling personality to steer them in the proper direction. This is what could happen, but need not happen if the right kind of a national Negro leader could at this time be gradually developed so as to overshadow Dr. King and be in the position to assume the role of the leadership of the Negro people when King has been completely discredited.

"For some months I have been thinking about this matter. One day I had an opportunity to explore this from a philosophical and sociological standpoint with [an acquaintance] whom I have known for some years.... I asked [him] to give the matter some attention and if he knew any Negro of outstanding intelligence and ability to let me know and we would have a discussion. [He] has submitted to me the name of the above-captioned person. Enclosed with this memorandum is an outline of [the person's] biography which is truly remarkable for a man so young. On scanning this biography, it will be seen that [he] does have all the qualifications of the kind of a Negro I have in mind to advance to positions of national leadership....

"If this thing can be set up properly without the Bureau in any way becoming directly involved, I think it would be not only a great help to the FBI but would be a fine thing for the country at large. While I am not specifying at this moment, there are various ways in which the FBI could give this entire matter the proper direction and development. There are highly placed contacts of the FBI who might be very helpful to further such a step. These can be discussed in detail later when I have probed more fully into the possibilities."

When Sullivan was shown this memorandum by the Committee, he testified:

"I'm very proud of this memorandum, one of the best memoranda I ever wrote. I think here I was showing some concern for the country."

Sullivan sought the Director's approval "to explore this whole matter in greater detail." The Director noted his own "o.k." and added:

"I am glad to see that 'light' has finally, though dismally delayed, come to the Domestic Int. Div. I struggled for months to get over the fact that the communists were taking over the racial movement but our experts here couldn't or wouldn't see it."

It is uncertain whether the FBI took steps to implement Sullivan's plan. The FBI files contain no additional memoranda on the subject. The successor for Dr. King proposed in Sullivan's memorandum has told the Committee that he was never contacted by the FBI, and that he was not aware of the FBI's plans for him or of any attempts by the FBI to promote him as a civil rights leader.

D. FBI Headquarters Orders the Field Offices To Intensify Efforts to Discredit Dr. King: April-August 1964

On April 1, 1964, in response to a suggestion from the Atlanta field office for another conference in Washington to plan strategy against Dr. King, FBI Headquarters ordered the Atlanta and New York offices to: "give the matter of instant investigation a thorough analysis with a view toward suggesting new avenues of investigation and intensification in areas already being explored. Bear in mind the main goals of this matter; namely, determining the extent of the communist influence in racial matters and taking such action as is appropriate to neutralize or completely discredit the effectiveness of Martin Luther King, Jr., as a Negro leader."

Headquarters listed several areas "having potential for further inquiry": "possibilities of anonymous source contacts, possibilities of utilizing contacts in the news media field, initiating discreet checks relative to developing background information on employees of the Southern Christian Leadership Conference (SCLC); remaining alert to the possibility of capitalizing on any disgruntled SCLC employee; the possibility of developing information concerning any financial dealings of King which may be illegal; and the development of subversive information pertaining to SCLC employees."

The Atlanta Office responded with several ideas for "how the effectiveness of King can be neutralized or discredited."

- Determining whether a "rift" was developing between Dr. King and Roy Wilkins, head of the NAACP, and if so, using newspapers friendly to the Bureau to "feed pertinent subversive connections and dealings of King to Wilkins."

- "Furnishing to friendly newspapers on an anonymous basis, certain specific leads where he may develop the necessary data so that he may further write critical news stories."

- "Discreetly investigate the background of twelve key (SCLC) employees and associates in an effort to obtain some weakness that could be used for counter-intelligence activities."

- "Injection of false information with certain discontented (SCLC) employees."

- Sending letters to SCLC's financial donors, written on SCLC stationery fabricated in the FBI laboratory and bearing Dr. King's signature, advising the donors that the IRS was checking SCLC's tax records. "It is believed that such a letter of this type from SCLC may cause considerable concern and eliminate future contributions."

- Placing a pretext call to an SCLC creditor to impress him with the "financial plight" of the SCLC so that he "may be incited into collection efforts."

- Examining Dr. King's checking accounts and credit card accounts to develop information about his financial affairs.

- Making a survey to determine whether to install a "trash cover" of the SCLC office in Atlanta.

The Atlanta office also assured the Bureau that it would continue to explore the possibility of technical coverage of an Atlanta apartment frequently used by Dr. King, although coverage would involve several security problems.

Shortly after these proposals were submitted, the Director expressed "the Bureau's gratitude" to the Atlanta agents for their "aggressive imagination looking toward more and better ways of meeting the problems involved" in the investigation.

The New York office submitted only a few new suggestions, asserting that "It is felt that [our] coverage is adequate." To this the Director replied:

"The Bureau cannot adjudge as adequate any coverage which does not positively provide to the Bureau 100 percent of the intelligence relating to the communist influence in racial matters. Obviously, we are not securing all the information that is pertinent and needs to be secured. Our coverage, therefore, is not deemed adequate."

With respect to the New York office's conclusions about a civil rights leader and associate of Dr. King, who was also under close Bureau scrutiny for alleged "subversive" ties, the Director wrote:

"The Bureau does not agree with the expressed belief of the New York office that [deleted] is not sympathetic to the Party cause. While there may not be any direct evidence that [deleted] is a communist, neither is there any substantial evidence that he is anticommunist."

Surprisingly, the Bureau did not even comment on the statement of the New York office that Adviser A was "not now under CP discipline in the civil rights field."

In June 1964 a special unit was established in the Bureau's Internal Security Section to handle exclusively "the over-all problem of communist penetration with the racial movement." The memorandum justifying the special unit pointed out that "urgency for the FBI to 'stay ahead' of the situation is tied to pending civil rights legislation and foreseeable ramifications arising out of the complex political situations in an election year where civil rights and social disturbances will play a key role in campaign efforts and possible election results."

In August the Bureau issued new instructions directing the field "to broaden its efforts relating to communist influences in the racial field." The term "communist," the field was told, "should be interpreted in its broadest sense as including persons not only adhering to the principles of the CPUSA itself, but also to such splinter and offshoot groups as the Socialist Workers Party, Progressive Labor and the like." The Director pointed out:

"The news media of recent months mirror the civil rights issue as probably the number one domestic issue in the political spectrum. There are clear and unmistakable signs that we are in the midst of a social revolution with the racial movement as its core. The Bureau, in meeting its responsibilities in this area, is an integral part of this revolution."

The Special Unit that had been established in June was made a permanent unit.

E. Steps Taken by the FBI in 1964 to Discredit Dr. King

The FBI's program to "neutralize" Martin Luther King as the leader of the civil rights movement went far beyond the planning and collection stage. The Committee has discovered the following attempts by the FBI to discredit Dr. King in 1964.

1. Attempts to Discredit Dr. King with the White House

As set forth in the preceding chapter, a memorandum summarizing the contents of the Willard Hotel tapes was shown to presidential assistant Walter Jenkins in January 1964 "inasmuch as King is seeking an appointment with President Johnson." The summary of information obtained from surveillance at the Willard, Honolulu, and Los Angeles hotels was sent to the White House and to the Attorney General in March 1964 in order to "remove all doubt from the Attorney General's mind as to the type of person King is." A third memorandum derived from microphone surveillance was sent to the White House in July.

2. Attempts to Discredit Dr. King With the Congress

In January 1964, Director Hoover gave off-the-record testimony before the House Appropriations Committee. His precise comments are not known. The briefing paper prepared for his appearance by the Domestic Intelligence Division, however, indicates that Director Hoover was prepared to represent to the Committee that Dr. King's advisers were communists and that Dr. King engaged in improper behavior.

The Director's off-the-record briefing had an immediate impact. The FBI was soon told that the members of the Committee were "very concerned regarding the background" of Dr. King, and that some members of the Committee felt that the President should be requested to instruct the USIA to withdraw a film dealing favorably with the August 1963 March on Washington. They were reported to be "particularly disturbed and irked at the fact that Martin Luther King appears to predominate the film."

In March 1964 Cartha DeLoach, Assistant to the Director, reported that he had been approached by Representative Howard Smith (D-Va.), Chairman of the House Rules Committee. According to DeLoach's memorandum, Representative Smith said that he had heard about the Director's remarks before the Appropriations Committee. Congressman Smith was reported to have asked for information for a speech about Dr. King on the floor of the House. DeLoach declined to furnish the required information, but recommended to the Director that Congressman Smith might be useful in the future because a speech by him about Dr. King would be picked up by "newspapers all over the Nation."

In a television interview several years later, Congressman Rooney stated:

"Now you talk about the FBI leaking something about Martin Luther King. I happen to know all about Martin Luther King, but I have never told anybody.

"INTERVIEWER. How do you know everything about Martin Luther King?

"Representative ROONEY. From the Federal Bureau of Investigation.

"INTERVIEWER. They've told you—gave you information based on tapes or other sources about Martin Luther King?

"Representative RODNEY. They did.

"INTERVIEWER. Is that proper?

"Representative ROONEY. Why not?"

3. Attempts to Discredit Dr. King with Universities

In early March 1964, the Bureau learned that Marquette University in Milwaukee, Wisconsin, contemplated awarding Dr. King an honorary degree. A memorandum noted:

"It is shocking indeed that the possibility exists that King may receive an Honorary Degree from the same institution which honored the Director with such a degree in 1950. . . . By making pertinent information available to [a University official] at this time, on a strictly confidential basis, we will be giving the University sufficient time to enable it to take positive action in a manner which might avoid embarrassment to the University."

The university official was briefed by an FBI agent on Dr. King's background and assured the Bureau that Dr. King would not be considered for an honorary degree. The result of this FBI project is unclear.

In April 1964, the FBI learned that Dr. King had been offered an honorary degree by Springfield College. DeLoach visited Senator Leverett Saltonstall, who was a member of the board of the College, in an effort to convince him to influence the College to withdraw its offer. According to DeLoach, Senator Saltonstall promised to speak with an official of the College. The College official was reported to have subsequently visited DeLoach, but to have said that he would be unable to "uninvite" Dr. King because the information concerning Dr. King had to be held in confidence, and the board of trustees was governed by "liberals."

4. Attempts to Discredit Dr. King with Churches

On June 12, 1964, William Sullivan wrote a memorandum stating that he had been contacted by the General Secretary of the National Council of the Churches of Christ. Sullivan reported that, "I took the liberty of advising [him] confidentially of the fact that Dr. Martin Luther King not only left a great deal to be desired from the standpoint of Communism, but also from the standpoint of personal conduct." Sullivan observed:

"I think that we have sowed an idea here which may do some good. I will follow up on the matter very discreetly to see what desirable results may emanate therefrom."

Sullivan met again with the General Secretary in mid-December 1964 and reported that the General Secretary had assured him "steps have been taken by the National Council of the Churches of Christ to make certain from this time on that Martin Luther King will never get 'one single dollar' of financial support from the National Council." Sullivan reported that the Secretary stated that he had discussed Dr. King's background with some "key" protestant clergymen who were "horrified." Sullivan also noted that the Secretary said that he also intended to discuss the matter with Roy Wilkins to persuade Wilkins "that Negro leaders should completely isolate King and remove him from the role he is now occupying in civil rights activities."

On December 8, 1964, the Director authorized the disclosure of information about Dr. King's personal life to an influential member of the Baptist World Alliance (BWA), so that he could pass the information along to the General Secretary of BWA, and to BWA Program Committee members, to prevent the Committee from inviting Dr. King to address the BWA's 1965 Congress in Miami Beach. The Director rejected a proposal, however, for "arranging for [certain BWA members] to listen to sources we have concerning this matter."

5. Attempts to Discredit Dr. King with the Pope

On August 31, 1964, the FBI learned that Dr. King, who was going to be touring Europe in September, might have plans to visit the Pope. Internal Security Section Chief Baumgardner observed:

"It would be shocking indeed for such an unscrupulous character as King to receive an audience with the Pope. It is believed that if a plan to see the Pope is in the making, it ought to be nipped in the bud. We have considered different possibilities for meeting this problem and believe that the best one would be to have Assistant Director Malone of the New York office personally contact Francis Cardinal Spellman and on a highly confidential basis bring to the Cardinal's attention the fact that King is to visit Rome.... Malone should be able to impress upon the Cardinal the likely embarrassment that may result to the Pope should he grant King an audience and King is later discredited."

On September 8, Baumgardner reported:

"Malone called today and stated that he had discussed the situation with Cardinal Spellman over the weekend and he said that the Cardinal took instant steps to advise the Vatican against granting any audience to King . . . Cardinal Spellman is going to Rome next week . . . and thus will be on the scene personally and further insure that the Pope is not placed in an embarrassing position through any contact with King."

The FBI's efforts were to no avail. The Pope met with Dr. King. The Director wrote across the memoranda informing him of that meeting, "astounding," and "I am amazed that the Pope gave an audience to such a [excised by FBI]." The Director then initiated inquiries into the reason for the failure of this project.

6. The Attempt to Discredit Dr. King During His Receipt of the Nobel Peace Prize

On October 14, 1964, Martin Luther King was named to win the Nobel Peace Prize. He received the prize in Europe on December 10, 1965. The FBI took measures to dampen Dr. King's welcome, both in Europe and on his return home.

On November 22, 1964 — two weeks before Dr. King's trip to receive the prize — the Domestic Intelligence Division assembled a thirteen-page updated printed version of the monograph which Attorney General Kennedy had ordered recalled in October 1963. A copy was sent to Bill Moyers, Special Assistant to the President, on December 1, 1964, with a letter requesting his advice concerning whether the monograph should also be distributed to "responsible officials in the Executive Branch." Moyers gave his permission on December 7, and copies were distributed to the heads of several executive agencies.

Information about Dr. King's private life was also made available to United Nations representatives Adlai Stevenson and Ralph Bunche, who the Bureau had learned were being considered as possible participants at the December 1964 "welcome home" reception for Dr. King.

Three days after Vice President-elect Humphrey participated in one of the "welcome home" receptions for Dr. King in New York, the Bureau sent him a copy of the updated King monograph and a separate memorandum entitled "Martin Luther King, Jr.: His Personal Conduct." On December 8, 1964, the Bureau decided to brief Governor Nelson Rockefeller about Dr. King's private life and alleged Communist associations, apparently to dissuade the Governor from taking part in ceremonies commending Dr. King for having received the Nobel Prize.

Upon learning that Dr. King might meet with a certain foreign leader, FBI headquarters instructed the FBI representative in that country to brief the proper authorities about Dr. King. The United States ambassadors in London and Oslo were briefed about Dr. King because "the Ambassadors might consider entertaining King while he is in Europe to receive the Nobel Peace Prize" and it might be possible to "forestall such action by the Ambassadors if they were briefed." The ambassadors in Stockholm and Copenhagen were also briefed because "King is also to visit those cities."

On November 10, 1964, the FBI learned that the United States Information Agency was considering requesting Dr. King to engage in a one-week lecture tour in Europe following his receipt of the Nobel Prize. Hoover approved the Domestic Intelligence Division's recommendation that USIA be furnished with the latest critical Bureau reports about Dr. King.

7. Attempts to Block Dr. King's Publications

On September 11, 1964, the FBI learned that Dr. King intended to publish an article in a major national publication.

The Domestic Intelligence Division noted that it did not know "what line King will take in the article or what its specific stands will be," but nonetheless recommended that "it would be well to prevent any publication of his views."

The task of preventing publication was assigned to an agent with contacts at the magazine who had "forestalled" the publication of an article by Dr. King in that magazine earlier in 1964.

The agent subsequently reported that he had contacted an official of the magazine in late September. According to the agent, the official had agreed to "endeavor to assist" the FBI, and had been briefed about King, but was unable to block publication because a contractual agreement had already been made. The FBI did apparently have some influence at the magazine, however, because a memorandum reporting the incident concludes:

"In connection with this [magazine] article by King, our sources have indicated that since he was awarded the Nobel Peace Prize he has attempted through some of his associates to change the [magazine] article in an effort to soften criticism made by him against other civil rights groups and leaders. King feared that such criticism would cause difficulties in the civil rights movement. The [magazine], however, has resisted King's efforts to make these changes."

In February 1964, the Director alerted the field offices that Dr. King was writing a new book, and noted that "it is entirely possible that with the publication of the book the Bureau may desire to take some action, possibly in the counterintelligence area or otherwise, which may be designed to discredit King or otherwise neutralize his effectiveness . . ."

The field offices were instructed to maintain information relating to the preparation and publication of the book. The FBI files indicate that this information was collected, but it is not clear whether it was ever used.

8. Attempt to Undermine the National Science Foundation's Cooperation with the SCLC

The FBI sent the National Science Foundation (NSF) a copy of the second printed monograph on King in order to convince the NSF to remove the SCLC from "the NSF program to obtain qualified Negro students from southern schools."

9. Unsuccessful FBI Attempts to Locate Financial Improprieties

In early January 1964, the Chief of the Internal Security Section of the Domestic Intelligence Division, Frederick J. Baumgardner, recommended that "examination of recent income tax returns of King might well reveal information which could assist the Bureau in its efforts to discredit King or neutralize his effectiveness." The Intelligence Division subsequently acquired from the Internal Revenue Service copies of income tax returns for the prior five years of Dr. King, the SCLC, and the Gandhi Society, an organization which the FBI stated "augmented" the fund-raising activities of the SCLC. The Intelligence Division of the IRS told the Bureau that "IRS had very carefully scrutinized King's returns in the past but had not been able to establish a cause of action against him." However, the IRS assured the FBI that Dr. King's current returns would be scrutinized "very carefully to determine whether any violations appear." None did.

Undeterred, the Director informed the field offices that "the Bureau believes that more than ever it would be most desirable to identify any bank where [King] may have an account ... and consider an audit of such account."

One effort to uncover derogatory information about Dr. King was conceived by the Supervisor in charge of the King case during a golf game. A remote acquaintance of the Supervisor mentioned that he had heard from a friend that an acquaintance had said that Dr. King had a numbered account in a foreign bank with a balance of over one million dollars. The Supervisor suggested to Sullivan:

"If we can prove that King is hoarding large sums of money, we would have available possibly the best information to date which could be used to discredit him, especially in the eyes of his own people . . . . we may take the action to discredit King ourselves through friendly news sources, or the like, or we might turn the information over to the Internal Revenue Service for possible criminal prosecution."

The plan was approved by Director Hoover and an inquiry was initiated. By December 1965, the investigation into a possible foreign bank account was described by the Director as "the most important presently pending" facet of the King investigation. The investigation was dropped shortly afterward, however, when it developed that the initial source of the allegation informed the FBI that "it was merely a wild conclusion that had been previously drawn by someone whose identity he does not now recall."

F. The Question of Whether Government Officials Outside of the FBI Were Aware of the FBI's Effort to Discredit Dr. King

There is no doubt that the responsible officials in the Kennedy and Johnson administrations were aware of the FBI's COMINFIL investigation involving Dr. King and the SCLC and that the wiretaps used by the FBI to collect its information were authorized under procedures existing at the time. While there is some question concerning whether officials outside of the FBI were aware that the FBI was using microphones to cover Dr. King's activities, there is no doubt that the product of the microphone surveillance was widely disseminated within the executive branch. Indeed, dissemination of the printed "monograph" about Dr. King to several executive agencies was expressly approved by Bill Moyers, President Johnson's assistant, in January 1965.

The Committee has been unable to determine the extent to which the FBI's effort to discredit Dr. King and the SCLC by disseminating unfavorable information outside of the Government was suspected or known about by Government officials responsible for supervising the FBI. The Committee requested the FBI to provide any information in its possession reflecting that any Presidents or Attorneys General during the relevant periods were aware of any FBI efforts to "discredit" or "neutralize" Dr. King. The Bureau replied:

"A review of the King file in response to other items included in the request and a polling of all Headquarters personnel involved in that and previous reviews did not result in the location or recollection of any information in FBIHQ files to indicate any of the aforementioned individuals were specifically aware of any efforts, steps or plans or proposals to 'discredit' or 'neutralize' King.

"It is, of course, evident that much information developed in the course of the King case involving him in activities of interest to the White House and to representatives of the Department of Justice, including Attorneys General Kennedy and Katzenbach, as well as Assistant Attorney General Marshall, was such that it could conceivably have been the opinion of one or more of the above individuals that such information was being provided to 'discredit' or 'neutralize' King."

Nicholas Katzenbach, Burke Marshall, Walter Jenkins, and Bill Moyers have told the Committee that they did not realize that the FBI was engaged in a concerted effort to discredit Dr. King, and that to the best of their knowledge, Presidents John Kennedy and Lyndon Johnson, as well as Attorney General Robert Kennedy, were not aware of that effort. There was no evidence that the FBI's program to discredit Dr. King was authorized outside of the FBI. There is evidence, however, that officials responsible for supervising the FBI received indications that such an effort to discredit Dr. King might be taking place, and failed to take adequate steps to prevent it. President Johnson and his Attorneys General were aware at least of Bureau attempts to disseminate unfavorable reports about Dr. King to the press. Top Executive Branch officials have told the Committee that they had believed that the FBI had tape recordings embarrassing to Dr. King, and that the FBI had offered to play those tapes both to a government official and to reporters. The evidence reveals a disturbing attitude of unconcern by responsible officials and a failure on their part to make appropriate corrective measures. As Nicholas Katzenbach explained to the Committee:

"Nobody in the Department of Justice connected with Civil Rights could possibly have been unaware of Mr. Hoover's feelings (against Dr. King). Nobody could have been unaware of the potential for disaster which those feelings embodied. But, given the realities of the situation, I do not believe one could have anticipated the extremes to which it was apparently carried."

The following incidents have played a part in our determination that high officials of the Executive Branch must share responsibility for the FBI's effort against Dr. King.

(1) As described in the previous chapter, a summary memorandum containing information gathered from the FBI microphone placed in Dr. King's room in the Willard hotel was shown to Presidential Assistant Walter Jenkins by Cartha DeLoach on January 14, 1964. According to DeLoach's contemporaneous account of that meeting:

"Jenkins was of the opinion that the FBI could perform a service to the country if this matter could somehow be confidentially given to members of the press. I told him the Director had this in mind, however, also believed we should obtain additional information prior to discussing it with certain friends."

DeLoach testified that he could not recall the meeting with Jenkins, but that the memorandum should accurately reflect his conversation.

Jenkins told the Committee staff in an unsworn interview that he did not recall the meeting described in DeLoach's memorandum, but that he had no reason to doubt that he had read the summary memorandum which DeLoach claims Jenkins saw. Jenkins expressly denied, however, that he had suggested that the information in the summary memorandum should be "leaked" to the press, or that either he or President Johnson had ever suggested that information about Dr. King should be "leaked" to anyone. He added, however, that he might have used words to the effect that "this is something people should know about"—referring to people in the Government—which could have been misinterpreted by DeLoach. He did not recall DeLoach telling him that the Director ultimately planned to leak this information to "certain friends."

(2) A February 5, 1964, FBI memorandum reports a conversation between Edwin Guthman, the Justice Department's press secretary, and John Mohr of the Domestic Intelligence Division. According to Mohr's memorandum, Guthman told Mohr that he had heard that a reporter was preparing an article about Dr. King's alleged Communist affiliations:

"Guthman stated he was quite concerned inasmuch as it appeared there had been a leak from the FBI in connection with this matter. He told me the Attorney General had been most hopeful that there would be no 'leaks' concerning King.

"From the tone of Guthman's entire remarks, it would appear he had two thoughts in mind without actually stating such thoughts. These, thoughts were (1) that the Attorney General is most anxious that information concerning King not be released; and (2) that the Attorney General's connections with King, and his defensive statements concerning King to Congress in Civil Rights hearings, would certainly injure the Attorney General's political chances for the future.

"(H)e told me once again the Attorney General was not worried about what an exposure of King could do to him. He stated he and the Attorney General are only trying to protect FBI sources of information."

The memorandum states that Guthman was told "there had been no leaks from the FBI concerning Dr. Martin Luther King," and that Guthman had responded that "he had no proof whatsoever that the FBI had furnished information to the newspapers concerning King."

Guthman testified that he recalled the Justice Department had "suspected that the information had been leaked by the FBI." When asked the basis for that suspicion, he said that "we felt that the question of King and the association with [Advisers A] was a matter which was rather tightly held since it was not something of general knowledge." Guthman said that he could "not specifically" recall a reaction by Attorney General Kennedy to this "leak": "except to be somewhat displeased over it, But that was in a sense all in a day's work and I don't recall anything specific."

Guthman testified that he did not recall any further efforts to determine whether the FBI had in fact leaked the story.

Guthman testified that DeLoach's memorandum "distorted" his remarks. Guthman said that his visit had been motivated, not by concerns about Kennedy's political future, but rather by a concern to protect FBI sources. A memorandum dated February 5, 1964, by Guthman, does not mention a meeting with Mohr, but does contain an account of a meeting between Guthman and Cartha DeLoach on the previous day:

"We both agreed that it was inevitable that King's connections with (Adviser A) would ultimately become public. I told DeLoach that our concern was over the FBI's source and that we had no other concern as to what the Attorney General had said or what our actions had been in connection with Martin Luther King.

"DeLoach said he thought we should be concerned in view of what the Attorney General had said on the subject. I pointed out that anything the Attorney General had said had been cleared with the FBI. I told Deke that our record in this matter could stand any scrutiny and that, both Senator Russell and Senator Monroney had been fully apprised of the facts last summer or last fall."

A memorandum by Courtney Evans later that day reports that Evans discussed this matter with Assistant Attorney General Burke Marshall, who said that he did not intend to tell the reporter anything about Dr. King, but that "if he developed anything at all with regard to [the reporter's] source of information, he would pass this along to us . . ." Evans' memorandum also notes, "According to information developed by our Atlanta office on February 4, 1964, [the reporter] had in his possession what appeared to be a blind memorandum containing information as to [Adviser A's alleged connections with the Communist Party]."

A memorandum from Cartha DeLoach to Director Hoover dated February 18, 1964, apparently alludes to this incident and provides some insight into the political implications of the FBI's investigation of Dr. King. According to DeLoach's memorandum, Walter Jenkins and Bill Moyers of the White House told him that Burke Marshall had called and "indicated that the Attorney General had thought it highly advisable for the President to see the Department of Justice file on Martin Luther King . . . to make certain that the President knew all about King."

The memorandum states that Marshall then: "told Moyers that he wanted to give the White House a little warning. He stated that he personally knew that the FBI had leaked information concerning Martin Luther King to a newspaper reporter. Marshall told Moyers that he thought the White House should know this inasmuch as information concerning King would undoubtedly be coming out before the public in the near future."

Director Hoover wrote next to this entry. "Marshall is a liar."

The memorandum reports that Jenkins told DeLoach that he thought the Attorney General was concerned with "being on record with the President with the fact that although he has, for political purposes, defended King, he wants the President to realize that he, the Attorney General, is well aware of King's Communistic background."

The Director's handwritten note states: "Katzenbach did his dirt against us before Warren Commission and now Marshall is trying to poison the W (hite) H (ouse) about FBI."

Neither Burke Marshall nor Bill Moyers recalled the events described in DeLoach's memorandum. Marshall testified, however, about an incident involving the FBI's leaking information to a reporter that may well have been the same incident. Marshall recalled that sometime in 1964, a reporter told him that the Atlanta office of the FBI had given him information unfavorable to Dr. King. Marshall said that he phoned the Bureau official with whom he normally conducted business and said, "I'm informed by a reporter that your people in Atlanta have given this information about Martin Luther King, and that I think it is outrageous." The official at first said, "I don't believe it," but promised to inquire further. He later called and said, "The Director wants you to know that you're a ... damned liar." Marshall told the Committee, "It was very difficult with the Bureau because if you said that they were leaking derogatory information, they would say, 'no, we're not.'"

(3) Bill Moyers, President Johnson's assistant, testified that sometime during the "hurley-burley disorganized period" shortly after President Kennedy's assassination and prior to President Johnson's state of the Union address, he heard laughter inside Walter Jenkins' office. Moyers inquired and was told by a secretary that an FBI agent had come to the office and offered to play for Jenkins a tape recording which would have been personally embarrassing to Dr. King. Jenkins refused to

listen to the tape. A week later, the same FBI agent again came to the White House and offered to play the tape for Jenkins, and again Jenkins refused to listen to it.

Jenkins told the Committee that he did not recall ever having been offered tapes by the FBI, and did not know of anyone on the White House staff who had been.

In addition to this incident, Moyers testified that he had been generally aware that the FBI reports about Dr. King included information of a personal nature, unrelated to the purpose of the FBI's investigation. When asked if he had ever asked the FBI why it was disseminating this type of material to the White House, Moyers responded:

"I don't remember. I just assumed it was related to a fallout of the investigations concerning the communist allegations, which is what the President was concerned about.

"Question. Did you ever question the propriety of the FBI's disseminating that type of information?

"Answer. I never questioned it, no. I thought it was spurious and irrelevant ... If they were looking for other alleged communist efforts to embarrass King and the President, which is what the President thought, Kennedy or Johnson, it would just seem natural that other irrelevant and spurious information would come along with that investigation.

"Question. And you found nothing improper about the FBI's sending that information along also?

"Answer. Unnecessary? Improper at that time, no.

"Question. Do you recall anyone in the White House ever questioning the propriety of the FBI's disseminating this type of material?

"Answer. I think there were comments that tended to ridicule the FBI's doing this, but no."

Moyers testified that he had not suspected that the FBI was covering Dr. King's activities with microphones, although he conceded, "I subsequently realized I should have assumed that. . . . The nature of the general references that were being made I realized later could only have come from that kind of knowledge unless there was an informer in Martin Luther King's presence a good bit of the time."

(4) According to Nicholas Katzenbach, on November 25, 1964, the Washington Bureau Chief of a national news publication told him that one of his reporters had been approached by the FBI and given an opportunity to listen to some "interesting" tapes involving Dr. King. Katzenbach told the Committee:

"I was shocked by this revelation, and felt that the President should be advised immediately. On November 28, I flew, with Mr. Burke Marshall, the retiring head of the Civil Rights Division, to the LBJ Ranch.

"On that occasion he and I informed the President of our conversation with the news editor and expressed in very strong terms our view that this was shocking conduct and politically extremely dangerous to the Presidency. I told the President my view that it should be stopped immediately and that he should personally contact Mr. Hoover. I received the impression that President Johnson took the matter very seriously and that he would do as I recommended.

"On the following Monday, I was informed by at least one other reporter, and perhaps two, of similar offers made to them the prior week. I spoke to the Bureau official who had been identified as having made the offer and asked him about it. He flatly denied that any such offer had been made or that the FBI would engage in any such activity. Thereupon I asked at least one of the reporters—perhaps all of them—whether they would join me in confronting the Bureau on this issue. They declined to do so.

"I do not know whether President Johnson discussed this matter with Mr. Hoover, or what, if anything, was said. However, I was quite confident that that particular activity ceased at that time, and I attributed it to Mr. Johnson's intervention. From that time until I left the Justice Department I never heard from any person of subsequent similar activity by the Bureau, and I assumed it had ceased. I should add only this: I believed that the tapes in question were not tapes resulting from Bureau surveillance but tapes acquired from State law enforcement authorities, and that such a representation was made to the reporter at the time."

Katzenbach testified that Cartha DeLoach was the Bureau official whom the reporters had identified as having offered the tapes. Katzenbach said that he had contacted DeLoach on his own volition, and that he did not tell DeLoach that he had discussed the matter with the President. He said that when he asked DeLoach if the Bureau had been offering to play tape recordings concerning Dr. King to reporters, DeLoach "told me rather angrily they were not."

Burke Marshall, when questioned by the Committee about these events, testified that the same two reporters had also informed him that Director Hoover was offering to play tape recordings of Dr. King. He testified that he had assumed the reporters "were telling the truth, that these tape recordings existed, and that they were being leaked by the FBI." He testified that he had not suspected that the FBI had produced the tapes itself from microphone coverage, but that he had assumed the FBI had acquired the tape recordings from Southern law enforcement agencies.

"It did not occur to me that the FBI would go around placing microphones in Dr. King's hotel . . . The notion that they would plant the microphone, that they had a whole system of surveillance of that sort, involving illegal entry and trespass and things like that, did not occur to me. I would not have put it past the local police, but I considered at the time—except for Mr. Hoover himself—that the Bureau was a tightly controlled, well-run, efficient, law abiding law enforcement agency, that it didn't do things like that, and therefore, it didn't occur to me that they had done it."

Marshall recalled that he and Katzenbach had flown to President Johnson's ranch in Texas and had told the President that the FBI was offering the tape recordings to reporters. Marshall said that the President, was "shocked," and that the "conversation was in the context of it being very important and a very nasty piece of business that had to be stopped." Marshall did not know, however, what action the President subsequently took, if any, and could not remember whether the President had voiced an intention to take any specific action.

DeLoach, when asked if he had ever discussed the contents of tape recordings or surveillances of Dr. King with members of the press, testified: "I don't recall any such conversations." DeLoach did state, however, that he had known about the tape recordings of Dr. King. He testified that one such tape recording had been in his office on one occasion, and that "it was so garbled and so terrible, I mean from the standpoint of fidelity, that I told them to knock it off and take it back."

The only record of this episode in the FBI files is a memorandum by DeLoach dated December 1, 1964, stating in part:

"Bill Moyers, while I was at the White House, today, advised that word had gotten to the President this afternoon that [the newsman] was telling all over town . . . that the FBI had told him that Martin Luther King was [excised]. [The newsman] according to Moyers, had stated to several people that, 'If the FBI will do this to Martin Luther King, they will undoubtedly do it to anyone for personal reasons.'

"Moyers stated the President wanted to get this word to us so we would know not to trust [the newsman]. Moyers also stated that the President felt that [the newsman] lacked integrity and was certainly no lover of the Johnson administration or the FBI. I told Moyers this was certainly obvious."

DeLoach testified that he could not recall the events surrounding this memorandum. Bill Moyers, after reviewing DeLoach's memorandum, testified that he recalled nothing about the incident involving the newsman or about Katzenbach's and Marshall's discussion with the President. He did not recall ever having heard that the Bureau had offered to play tape recordings of Dr. King to reporters, or ever having discussed the matter with DeLoach. He testified, however, that DeLoach's memorandum: "sounds very plausible. I'm sure the President called me or he told me to tell him whatever [DeLoach's document reflects].

"Question. Did the President tell you that he understood that [the newsman] was saying all over town that the Bureau had been offering tapes?

"Answer. I can't remember the details of that. You know, I can't tell you the number of times the President was sounding off at [the newsman]."

When asked if it would be fair to conclude that the President had complained to Moyers about the newsman's revealing that the Bureau had offered to play tapes rather than about the fact that the Bureau had such tapes and had offered to play them, Movers replied, "It would be fair to conclude that. I don't recall if that was exactly the way the President said it."

VI. The Hoover-King Controversy Becomes Public And A Truce Is Called: April-December 1964

Summary

Director Hoover's dislike for Dr. King, which had been known within the Bureau since early 1962, became a matter of public record in November 1964 when Director Hoover described Dr. King at a meeting with women reporters as the "most notorious liar" in the country. Dr. King responded that the Director was obviously "faltering" under the responsibilities of his office. The FBI immediately intensified its secret campaign against Dr. King, offering to play the tapes from microphone surveillance of Dr. King to reporters and to leak stories concerning him to the press. The FBI also sent a tape recording made from the microphone surveillance to Dr. King, with a warning which Dr. King and his close associates interpreted as an invitation to suicide.

The public aspects of the dispute peaked in December 1964, shortly before Dr. King went to Europe to receive the Nobel Peace Prize. Dr. King publicly announced that it was time for the controversy to end, and arranged a meeting with Director Hoover to seal a truce. The FBI's public criticism stopped, but the Bureau's secret campaign to discredit Dr. King continued. Believing that Dr. King's downfall would severely harm the entire movement for racial equality, several prominent civil rights figures met with FBI officials to voice their concern and seek assurances from the FBI that the attacks on Dr. King would stop.

A. First Steps in the Public Controversy April-November 1964

Although the FBI had been covertly engaged in a massive campaign to discredit Dr. King for several months, the fact that the FBI was the source of allegations about communist influence in the civil rights movement did not become public until the release of Director Hoover's off-the-record testimony before the House Appropriations Committee in April 1964. The Director was quoted in the press as having testified that "'Communist influence does exist in the Negro movement" and can influence "large masses of people.'" Dr. King immediately issued a forceful reply:

"It is very unfortunate that Mr. J. Edgar Hoover, in his claims of alleged communist infiltration in the civil rights movement, has allowed himself to aid and abet the salacious claims of southern racists and the extreme right-wing elements.

"We challenge all who raise the 'red' issue, whether they be newspaper columnists or the head of the FBI himself, to come forward and provide real evidence which contradicts this stand of the SCLC. We are confident that this cannot be done.

"We affirm that SCLC is unalterably opposed to the misguided philosophy of communism.

"It is difficult to accept the word of the FBI on communist infiltration in the civil rights movement, when they have been so completely ineffectual in resolving the continued mayhem and brutality inflicted upon the Negro in the deep south. It would be encouraging to us if Mr. Hoover and the FBI would be as diligent in apprehending those responsible for bombing churches and killing little children as they are in seeking out alleged communist infiltration in the civil rights movement."

In early May 1964, Director Hoover made the following response to a question from United Press International concerning whether any communists were in positions of leadership in the civil rights movement:

"Let me first emphasize that I realize the vast majority of Negroes have rejected and recognize communism for what it is.

"The existence and importance of the communist influence in the Negro movement should not be ignored or minimized, nor should it be exaggerated. The Communist Party will use its forces either in the open forum of public opinion or through its sympathizers who do not wear the badge of communism but who spout some of the same ideas carried in the Communist Party line. This is the influence which is capable of moving large masses of loyal and dedicated citizens toward communist objectives while being lured away from the true issues involved. It is up to the civil rights organizations themselves to recognize this and face up to it."

On May 11, Dr. King appeared on the news program, *Face the Nation*. He denied communists had infiltrated decision-making positions in the civil rights movement or the SCLC and remarked that it was "unfortunate" that "such a great man" as Director Hoover had made allegations to that effect. Dr. King added that the Director should more appropriately have remarked on how surprising it was that so few Negroes had turned to communism in light of the treatment they had received. Dr. King said that the Justice Department had warned him of only one suspected communist in the SCLC, and that he had fired that individual.

The feud between Director Hoover and Dr. King heightened on November 18, 1964, with the Director's public allegation that Dr. King was the "most notorious liar" in the country. Director Hoover made that comment during a meeting with women reporters in the context of explaining how FBI agents were assigned in civil rights cases. According to a memorandum of the meeting written by DeLoach:

"[The Director] stated it was a common belief in some circles that Special Agents in the South were all, without exception, southern born agents. As a matter of fact, 70% of the agents currently assigned to the South were born in the North. He stated that the 'notorious' Martin Luther King had attempted to capitalize on this matter by claiming that all agents assigned to the Albany, Georgia, Resident Agency were southern born agents. As a matter of fact, 4 out of 5 of the agents assigned to the Albany, Georgia, Resident Agency were northern born. The Director stated he had instructed me to get in touch with Reverend King and line up an appointment so that King could he given the true facts. He stated that King had refused to give me an appointment and, therefore, he considered King to be the most 'notorious liar' in the country."

When the reporters asked Director Hoover for more details about Dr. King, "he stated, off the record, 'He is one of the lowest characters in the country.' There was an immediate inquiry as to whether he could be quoted on the original statement that Martin Luther King was a liar and he stated, 'Yes — that is public record.' "

Nicholas Katzenbach, who was then Acting Attorney General, testified that he talked with Director Hoover about that press conference and "[Hoover] told me that it was not his practice to have press conferences, had not done so in the past, and would not do so again in the future. Perhaps the depth of his feeling with respect to Dr. King was revealed to me by his statement that he did not understand all the publicity which the remark had attracted because he had been asked a simple question and given a simple truthful answer."

Some of Dr. King's advisers drafted a strong response, one of which would have "blown Hoover out of the water, calling him every name in the book." Before they had an opportunity to release the statement, Dr. King, who was then in Bimini, issued the following public reply:

"I cannot conceive of Mr. Hoover making a statement like this without being under extreme pressure. He has apparently faltered under the awesome burden, complexities and responsibilities of his office."

Dr. King also sent a telegram to Director Hoover, which was made public, stating:

"I was appalled and surprised at your reported statement maligning my integrity. What motivated such an irresponsible accusation is a mystery to me.

"I have sincerely questioned the effectiveness of the F.B.I. in racial incidents, particularly where bombings and brutalities against Negroes are at issue . . .

"I will be happy to discuss this question with you at length in the near future. Although your statement said you have attempted to meet with me, I have sought in vain for any record of such a request."

Dr. King also criticized Director Hoover in a press interview on the same day for "following the path of appeasement of political powers in the South."

The Domestic Intelligence Division prepared an analysis of the allegations in Dr. King's telegram, emphasizing the events two years earlier which the FBI had interpreted as a refusal by Dr. King to be interviewed. Sullivan recommended against replying to Dr. King's charges or meeting with Dr. King. The Director penned his agreement on Sullivan's memorandum:

"O.K. But I can't understand why we are unable to get the true facts before the public. We can't even get our accomplishments published. We are never taking the aggressive, but above lies remain unanswered."

The following day, the FBI mailed a tape recording from the Willard Hotel microphone surveillance to Dr. King accompanied by a letter which Dr. King and his associates interpreted as an invitation to suicide.

B. Tapes Are Mailed to King: November 21, 1964

Sometime in mid-November 1964 a decision was made at FBI Headquarters to mail a tape recording made during microphone surveillance of Dr. King to the SCLC office in Atlanta. William Sullivan, who was responsible for the project, testified that he first learned of the plan when Alan Belmont, Assistant to the Director, told him that Director Hoover wanted one of the King tapes mailed to Coretta King to precipitate their separation, thereby diminishing Dr. King's stature. Belmont told Sullivan that the FBI laboratory would "sterilize the tape to prevent its being traced to the Bureau." Sullivan was to have the tape mailed from a southern state.

Sullivan told the Committee that he had opposed the plan because it would warn Dr. King that his activities were being covered by microphones. According to Sullivan, Belmont agreed that the plan was unwise, but said that he had no power to stop it because the orders had come from Hoover and Tolson.

The FBI technician who prepared the tape told the Committee that he had been ordered to produce a "composite" tape from coverage of hotel rooms in Washington, D.C., San Francisco, and Los Angeles. After the tape was completed, a copy was left with Sullivan.

Sullivan testified that he ordered a "tight-lipped . . . reliable" agent to fly to Tampa, Florida, to mail a package to Coretta

King. He did not tell the agent that the package contained the King tape. The agent testified that he flew to Miami and then called Sullivan, who instructed him to address the package to Martin Luther King, Jr. The agent said that he mailed the package from a post office near the Miami airport. A travel voucher provided to the Committee by the FBI indicates that the agent flew to Miami on November 21, 1964.

Congressman Andrew Young, who was then Dr. King's assistant, recalled that the tape arrived at the SCLC Headquarters in Atlanta sometime before December 1964. Congressman Young said that the office personnel assumed the tape contained another of Dr. King's speeches; it was stored for a while, and later sent to Dr. King's home along with several other tapes. Dr. King, Congressman Young, and some others listened to the tape sometime after Dr. King had returned from receiving the Nobel Peace Prize, probably in January 1965. Congressman Young testified that he probably destroyed the tape several years later.

Congressman Young recalled that the tape was of "very poor quality, very garbled," but that at least part of it appeared to have been made during a conversation between Dr. King and other civil rights leaders at the Willard Hotel. He testified that none of the comments on the tape related to the commission of a crime or to "affection" for communism. "It was personal conversation among friends."

According to Congressman Young a letter had accompanied the tape, stating that the tape would be released in 34 days and threatening "there is only one thing you can do to prevent this from happening." Congressman Young said that when he and Dr. King read the letter, "we assumed that the letter and the tape had been mailed 34 days before the receipt of the Nobel Prize, and that this was a threat to expose Martin just before he received the Nobel Prize." Congressman Young testified:

"I think that the disturbing thing to Martin was that he felt somebody was trying to get him to commit suicide, and because it was a tape of a meeting in Washington and the postmark was from Florida, we assumed nobody had the capacity to do that other than the Federal Bureau of Investigation."

Both Young and Ralph Abernathy, who also heard the tape and read the letter, interpreted it as inviting Dr. King to take his own life.

William Sullivan testified that he could not recall such a letter. The FBI provided the Committee with a copy of a letter which was found in Sullivan's office files following his discharge in 1971. The letter stated in part:

"King, look into your heart. You know you are a complete fraud and a greater liability to all of us Negroes. White people in this country have enough frauds of their own but I am sure they don't have one at this time that is anywhere near your equal. You are no clergyman and you know it. I repeat that you are a colossal fraud and an evil, vicious one at that....

"King, like all frauds your end is approaching. You could have been our greatest leader. . . . But you are done. Your 'honorary' degrees, your Nobel Prize (what a grim farce) and other awards will not save you. King, I repeat you are done....

"The American public, the church organizations that have been helping—Protestants, Catholics and Jews will know you for what you are—an evil beast. So will others who have backed you. You are done.

"King, there, is only one thing left for you to do. You know what it is. You have just 34 days in which to do (this exact number has been selected for a specific reason, it has definite practical significance). You are done. There is but one way out for you. You better take it before your filthy fraudulent self is bared to the nation."

Andrew Young stated that the last paragraph of this letter was identical with the letter that had been sent to the SCLC headquarters, but that the other portions of the letter appeared to be an earlier draft of the letter that he had seen. Sullivan testified that he did not recall ever having seen the document, although it was "possible" that he had something to do with it and simply cannot remember. Sullivan also testified that he could not recall any conversations at the FBI concerning the possibility of Dr. King's committing suicide. After reading the last paragraph of the letter, he conceded that it could be interpreted as an invitation to suicide, although so far as Sullivan knew, the FBI's goal was simply to convince Dr. King to resign from the SCLC, not to kill himself.

When asked by the Committee what had ultimately happened to the letter received by Reverend King, Andrew Young testified:

"I'm not really sure about this now, but I think we discussed something about a letter with DeLoach — I'm not certain whether it was DeLoach or the local FBI agents — and they said they would be glad to look into it. They said, whenever we got any of these kind of threatening letters, to send them to them, and they would be glad to investigate. That letter may have been sent back to DeLoach."

C. Attempts by the FBI to "Leak" to Reporters Tape Recordings Embarrassing to Dr. King

After Director Hoover denounced Dr. King as a "notorious liar" in mid-November, the FBI apparently made several attempts to "leak" tape recordings concerning Dr. King to newsmen. One offer involving the Bureau Chief of a national news publication has been discussed at length in the preceding chapter. David Kraslow, another reporter, has told a Committee staff member, that one of his "better sources at the Bureau" offered him a transcript of a tape recording about Dr. King. Kraslow said that his source read him a portion of the transcript on the phone, and claimed that it came from a "bug" operated by a Southern police agency. Kraslow said that he declined the offer.

It is not known how many other reporters were approached by the FBI during that period; Nicholas Katzenbach testified that at least one other reporter had informed him of a similar Bureau offer, and other witnesses, such as James Farmer, have mentioned additional "leaks" from the Bureau.

D. Roy Wilkins of NAACP meets with DeLoach to discuss allegations about Dr. King: November 27, 1994

On November 24, 1964, Director Hoover gave a speech at Loyola University in Chicago in which he referred to moral laxness in civil rights groups. On November 27, Roy Wilkins, Executive Secretary of NAACP, phoned DeLoach and requested a meeting. Wilkins told the Committee that he had been disturbed by Hoover's Loyola University speech a few days before, and that he had realized Hoover had been referring to Dr. King because of rumors then circulating that the FBI had developed "derogatory" material about Dr. King. Wilkins was spurred into meeting with DeLoach by pointed inquiries from several reporters about whether Director Hoover's remarks had been directed toward Dr. King. Wilkins described his motivation in requesting the meeting as "protecting the civil rights movement." He said that Dr. King did not learn of his meeting with DeLoach until over a week after it had occurred.

DeLoach and Wilkins have given the Committee differing accounts of what was said at their meeting. DeLoach's version is summarized in a letter that he sent to President Johnson on November 30, 1964:

"Wilkins said that ... the ruination of King would spell the downfall of the entire civil rights movement ... Wilkins indicated that [if allegations concerning King's personal conduct and supposed connections with communists were publicized], many of his Negro associates would rise to his defense. He felt, however, that many white people who believe in the civil rights movement and who yearly contribute from $500 to $50,000 to this movement would immediately cease their financial support. This loss, coupled with the loss of faith in King by millions of Americans, would halt any further progress of the civil rights movement."

A memorandum by DeLoach written shortly after the meeting states:

"I told him ... that if King wanted war we certainly would give it to him. Wilkins shook his head and stated there was no doubt in his mind as to which side would lose if the FBI really came out with all its ammunition against King. I told him the ammunition was plentiful and that while we were not responsible for the many rumors being initiated against King, we had heard of these rumors and were certainly in a position to substantiate them."

DeLoach's memorandum stated that the meeting had concluded with Wilkins' promise to "tell King that he can't win in a battle with the FBI and that the best thing for him to do is to retire from public life."

Wilkins told the Committee that DeLoach's description of the meeting was "self serving and filled with inaccuracies" and denied DeLoach's description of his remarks as "pure invention." Wilkins stated that he had expressed his concern that accusations about Dr. King would cripple the civil rights movement, noting that if charges were publicly levied against Dr. King, the black community would side with Dr. King and the white community with Director Hoover. Wilkins said that he advised DeLoach that the FBI should not overreact to Dr. King's criticisms and that he considered Dr. King's criticism of the FBI's failure to vigorously enforce the civil rights laws to be totally justified. Wilkins told the Committee that although he had considered the meeting a "success" at the time, after reading DeLoach's memorandum he realized that he had failed to convey the impression that he had intended, since DeLoach had clearly misinterpreted his remarks.

When DeLoach was asked by the Committee if the "ammunition" he had threatened to use against Dr. King was the tape recordings, DeLoach replied, "I don't know what I had in mind, frankly, it's been so long ago, I can't recall." Wilkins did not remember DeLoach's use of the term "ammunition," but did recall that DeLoach frequently alluded to "derogatory information," although Wilkins was unclear whether DeLoach was referring to allegations about Dr. King's personal conduct or about Communist infiltration of the SCLC.

The following day, an official of the Domestic Intelligence Division proposed to William Sullivan, head of the Division, that several leading members of the Black community should be briefed about Dr. King by the FBI "on a highly confidential basis." It was proposed that "the use of a tape, such as contemplated in your memorandum, together with a transcript for convenience in following the tape," should be used.

"The inclusion of U.S. Government officials, such as Carl Rowan or Ralph Bunch, is not suggested as they might feel a duty to advise the White House of such contemplated meeting. . . . This group should include such leadership as would be capable of removing King from the scene if they, of their own volition, decided this was the thing to do after such a briefing."

E. Dr. King and Director Hoover Meet: December 1, 1964

According to one of Dr. King's legal counsels, Harry Wachtel, several prominent civil rights leaders told Dr. King of their concern that public controversy with Director Hoover would hurt the civil rights movement, but promised to support Dr. King should such a confrontation occur. Wachtel recalled that Dr. King and his staff pondered "how to defuse this and prevent it from becoming the principal focus of the struggle, Hoover versus King," which "could only have lead to a division and thus a dilution of the growing strength of the civil rights movement." Wachtel testified:

"Everything pointed toward the problem of how Hoover would respond if Dr. King said in effect, 'you're a liar; prove your case. If you call me a liar, prove it.' Every lawyer worth his salt knows this is the beginning of the Alger Hiss type of dilemma. Libel and slander litigation or public debate of famous personalities can easily lead to destruction of an ongoing movement. You end up spending your time fighting over 'truth as a defense.' "

Dr. King and his advisers settled on an approach to the problem, and on the evening of November 30, 1964, at a public meeting in honor of his receiving the Nobel Peace Prize, Dr. King announced his intention to meet with Director Hoover to iron out their differences:

"I do not plan to engage in public debate with Mr. Hoover and I think the time has come for all this controversy to end, and for all of us to get on with the larger job of civil rights and law enforcement."

According to Andrew Young, who was then Dr. King's Executive Assistant, the meeting was arranged by Dr. Archibald Carey, a close friend of both DeLoach and Dr. King, at King's request.

Young recalled that Dr. King had been surprised by Director Hoover's "most notorious liar" allegation and wanted to find out what was at the heart of the problem. Walter Fauntroy, who said that his recollection of events surrounding the meeting was "fuzzy," added that Dr. King had also been motivated by a desire to bring to the Director's attention complaints of Southern SCLC workers concerning the lack of FBI protection during civil rights demonstrations.

The meeting between Dr. King and Director Hoover took place at 3:30 p.m. on the afternoon of December 1, 1964. Dr. King was accompanied by Ralph Abernathy, Secretary of the SCLC; Andrew Young, Dr. King's Executive Assistant; and Walter Fauntroy, the SCLC representative in Washington. Director Hoover was accompanied by Cartha DeLoach.

DeLoach detailed the meeting in a twelve-page memorandum which Young and Abernathy described as "substantially" accurate, finding fault chiefly with the praise of

Director Hoover and of the FBI which DeLoach attributed to Dr. King. According to the DeLoach account, Dr. King said: "(he) wanted to clear up any misunderstanding which might have occurred. He stated that some Negroes had told him that the FBI had been ineffective, however, he was inclined to discount such criticism. Reverend King asked that the Director please understand that any criticism of the Director and the FBI which had been attributed to King was either a misquote or an outright misrepresentation. He stated this particularly concerned Albany, Georgia. ...

"Reverend King stated he personally appreciated the great work of the FBI which had been done in so many instances ... Reverend King stated he has never made any personal attack upon Mr. Hoover ... Reverend King said that the Director's report to the President this summer on rioting was a very excellent analysis.

"Reverend King stated he has been and still is very concerned regarding the matter of communism in the civil rights movement. Reverend King stated that from a strong philosophical point of view he could never become a communist ... He claimed that when he learns of the identity of a communist in his midst he immediately deals with the problem by removing this man. He stated there have been one or two communists who were engaged in fundraising for the SCLC. Reverend King then corrected himself to say that these one or two men were former communists and not Party members at the present time ... He stated that he had insisted that [Adviser B] leave his staff because the success of his organization ... was far more important than friendship with [Adviser B]."

According to Young, the meeting opened with a simple exchange of greetings—not with the excessive praise of the Director reflected in DeLoach's memorandum—and then Director Hoover proceeded to give a monologue that lasted for some fifty-five minutes. DeLoach's summary memorandum bears out Young's characterization of the meeting as essentially a briefing by Director Hoover on FBI operations relating to civil rights.

Congressman Young testified that neither the Director's pointed criticism of Dr. King nor the possibility that the FBI was spreading rumors about Dr. King was raised at the meeting. Neither Young nor Abernathy recalled any hint of blackmail, but Abernathy did remember quite clearly that at one point Hoover "gave King a lecture reminding him that he was a man of the cloth" and a national leader, and that he should "behave himself." Abernathy did not discern any hint that Dr. King had not lived up to the expected standards. He said that Dr. King remained "very calm," thanked Director Hoover for the reminder, and agreed that it was important for a national leader to set a moral example. Abernathy said that the Director then told Dr. King, "If you haven't done anything wrong, you don't have anything to worry about."

Although DeLoach's memorandum of the meeting states that Director Hoover and Dr. King discussed possible Communist influence in the SCLC, Andrew Young testified:

"He never brought up the subject of Communism at all . . . (Adviser A's) name never came up, and there was never any discussion in our meeting about Communism or Communist advisers."

DeLoach described the meeting to the Committee as follows:

"I fully expected it to be a confrontation. However, to the contrary, it was more or less of a love feast with Mr. Hoover telling Dr. King that Dr. King is a symbol of leadership for 12 million Negroes and should be careful about his associations and about his personal conduct, and Dr. King telling Mr. Hoover that he had not wished to cast any reflection upon the FBI and had no intention of doing so in the future. In other words, it was a very peaceful meeting."

Andrew Young agreed that there had been "not even an attitude of hostility. In fact, Hoover was very disarming in that he congratulated Dr. King for having won the Nobel Prize, and as far as we are concerned, this was not the same man that called Martin a notorious liar. We attributed it to the fact of his age and the kinds of possible fluctuations that are possible with people under pressure in advanced years."

Young also told the Committee that within a few weeks of the meeting, the FBI announced that it had arrested suspects in the summer murder of three civil rights workers in the South. "So in a sense we were reassured that the FBI was doing its law enforcement job, and we hoped the personal tensions, as far as Dr. King was concerned, were over and done."

Harry Wachtel said that Dr. King and his advisors had viewed the meeting as a success because it had "defused" the FBI's attacks in time to permit Dr. King to travel to Europe and receive the Nobel Prize. Wachtel believed that Dr. King's response to Hoover's challenge prevented the FBI from succeeding in what Wachtel viewed as an attempt to promote disputes and factionalism among the civil rights leaders:

"The factionalism that the FBI sought to create was widespread. It came out in the Committee's record that they were even seeking a new leader. In CIA terms, you find yourself a new president of a country who is in your control ... They were applying to domestic affairs the type of factionalism that they had worked on so successfully.... And you had to be around to know that it didn't take much to disrupt this delicate marriage of the leadership of the civil rights movement."

A memorandum written by DeLoach on December 12, 1964, indicates that the FBI also viewed the feud with Dr. King as having quieted. In response to an inquiry from William Sullivan concerning whether the remainder of the tape recordings about Dr. King should be transcribed, DeLoach responded:

"I fully agree that the work should eventually be done, particularly if an additional controversy arises with King. I see no necessity, however, in this work being done at the present time inasmuch as the controversy has quieted down considerably and we are not in need of transcripts right now ... I would recommend that we hold off doing this tremendous amount of work until there is an actual need."

F. Civil Rights Leaders Attempt To Dissuade the FBI From Discrediting Dr. King: December 1964 - May 1965

1. Farmer-DeLoach Meeting: December 1, 1964

On December 1, 1964—apparently immediately following Hoover's meeting with Dr. King—James Farmer, National Director of the Congress of Racial Equality, met with DeLoach to convince him not to launch a smear campaign against Dr. King. Farmer explained the circumstances leading up to the meeting to the Committee as follows.

During the last week in November 1964, Farmer met with the editor of a New York newspaper who said that he had been with an FBI agent when Director Hoover's accusation of Dr. King as a "notorious liar," was reported. The editor told Farmer that the Agent had remarked, "the Chief has finally gotten it off his chest." The Agent then went into a "tirade" against Dr. King. A few days later, Farmer was told by a reporter from the New York *Post* that stories about Dr. King were being repeated in journalistic circles. Shortly afterwards, Farmer was informed that a conservative columnist was preparing a derogatory story about Dr. King, and that the FBI was prepared to back up his allegations.

Farmer told the Committee that a CORE staff member had verified this rumor with an FBI contact who reportedly said "the chief wants Farmer to know" that he had no interest in "getting Farmer, Whitney Young, or Roy Wilkins—only King."

Farmer then called DeLoach, whom he considered to be a "man of his word," and asked for a private conference. Before the meeting, Farmer met with Dr. King and told him about the allegations. Dr. King approved Farmer's meeting with DeLoach, but did not tell Farmer that he was intending to meet with Director Hoover.

On December 1, Farmer conferred with DeLoach in the back seat of a limousine while driving around Washington, D.C. Farmer told the Committee that DeLoach began the conversation by remarking, "I know why you wanted to come down here." He recalled that DeLoach said that the FBI did have evidence which supported the rumors about Dr. King, but that the Bureau was not "peddling" the information.

DeLoach's memorandum of that meeting states:

"Farmer told me that he had heard from a number of newsmen that the FBI planned to expose Reverend King by tomorrow, Wednesday, December 2, 1964. He stated that he and King had had a lengthy conference last night in New York City and that it had been agreed that Farmer should come down to see me and prevent this action being taken if at all possible. He stated he knew that King had made a sudden decision to come down also and that he hoped that King's meeting with the Director had been an amiable one. I told him that it had been.

"I told Farmer that we, of course, had no plan whatsoever to expose Reverend King. I told him that our files were sacred to us and that it would be unheard of for the FBI to leak such information to newsmen. I told him I was completely appalled at the very thought of the FBI engaging in such endeavors....

"I again repeated that we had never entertained the idea to expose Reverend King; however, I wanted Farmer to definitely know that the campaign of slander and vilification against the Director and the FBI should stop without any delay. I told him that if this war continued that we, out of necessity, must defend ourselves. I mentioned that I hoped it would not be necessary for the FBI to adopt defensive tactics. Farmer got the point without any difficulty whatsoever. He immediately assured me that there would be no further criticism from him. He stated he felt certain there would be no further criticism from King."

Farmer was shown DeLoach's memorandum by the Committee. He denied that he had assured DeLoach that his or

Dr. King's criticism of the FBI would cease, that there had been any discussion of "warfare," and he stated that he did not know what the reference to his "getting the point" meant.

2. Young-Abernathy-DeLoach Meeting: January 8, 1965

On January 8, 1965—shortly after the tape and letter were brought to the attention of the leaders of the SCLC—Andrew Young and Ralph Abernathy, at Dr. King's urgings, requested a meeting with Director Hoover.

Both Young and Abernathy told the Committee that the purpose of the meeting was to determine why the FBI was antagonistic toward Dr. King and to stem continuing attacks against Dr. King's character. Young said that the meeting was prompted by the receipt of the tape and letter. Abernathy confirmed this account, and added that although they had not assumed that the FBI had sent the tape itself, they did believe that the FBI had at least known about the tape and could help in terminating the campaign of personal abuse directed against Dr. King.

DeLoach, rather than Director Hoover, met with Young and Abernathy. Abernathy told the Committee that he had made it unmistakably clear to DeLoach they were concerned about charges bearing on Dr. King's personal conduct. DeLoach's memorandum of the meeting states:

"Reverend Abernathy spoke very generally, pointing out that people were always 'making charges' and 'innuendoes' against Mr. King.... Reverend Young said it looked like there were some attempts to smear and ruin the civil rights movement; that just lately there has been some new evidence in this regard and that very obviously the activities of Mr. King and the SCLC are under close surveillance....

"[Young] said he did feel though there must be some sort of concerted organized campaign that was being directed against King and the SCLC....

"Reverend Abernathy stated that there were three points they had wanted to discuss; communist infiltration, allegations that King was getting rich on the civil rights movement, and the third point had to do with allegations about the personal life and moral character of King.... Abernathy said that he was not going to make allegations against the FBI but that some things were going on they just could not understand.

"Reverend Young said that King had been receiving letters charging him with immorality, that these letters attacked his personal life.

"Reverend Young said that he was deeply concerned about irresponsible usage of personal information on the part of scandalmongers and wondered if there could be any 'leaks' from the Government. He was assured that there were no leaks from the FBI, that the Director ran a tight organization and that any irresponsibility on the part of any agent would not be tolerated."

Andrew Young testified that he "thought" that he had mentioned the letter and tape recording that had been received by Dr. King. He recalled that DeLoach "denied everything. He denied that an FBI agent would ever talk to the press about anything."

"Question. Did you bring up the issue of whether the FBI was tapping Dr. King's phone, SCLC's phone, or bugging Dr. King?

"YOUNG. Yes, we did. He assured us that was not true."

3. Carey-DeLoach Meeting. — May 19, 1965

On May 19, 1965, Dr. Archibald J. Carey, Jr., then a Chicago attorney who was well acquainted with Dr. King, DeLoach, and Director Hoover, met with DeLoach to "mediate" in what he regarded as an unfortunate dispute among his friends. Dr. Carey told the Committee staff that Dr. King had first brought to his attention rumors about Dr. King's "communist sympathies" and personal conduct during a weekend visit to Chicago some time in May 1965. On that occasion, Dr. King told Dr. Carey that the FBI was trying to discredit him and might release stories to the press regarding his personal life in the near future. Dr. Carey told the Committee that Dr. King did not ask him to talk with the FBI about their attempt to discredit him, but rather that he had volunteered to "see what he could do." Dr. King gave his assent.

DeLoach, in a memorandum of the meeting, wrote that "Carey told me that he wanted to enlist the sympathies of the FBI in not letting any effort to discredit King occur." DeLoach said that he had told Dr. Carey that "the FBI had plenty to do without being responsible for a discrediting campaign against Reverend King." DeLoach ended the memorandum with the comment:

"Dr. Carey is the third individual that King has had come to see us relative to requesting that we not expose him. Roy Wilkins, Jim Farmer, and Reverend Abernathy have all been here for the same purpose. It is obvious that King is becoming very disturbed and worried about his background, else he would not go to such great efforts to have people approach the FBI. I did not commit the FBI in any manner insofar as exposing King is concerned. To the contrary, I let Carey flatly know of King's derelictions insofar as false allegations against us are concerned and of the fact that King and other civil rights workers owed the FBI a debt of gratitude they would never be able to repay."

Director Hoover wrote on the memorandum, "Well handled."

Dr. Carey told the Committee staff that he contacted Dr. King after the meeting and suggested that criticizing the FBI was not the best strategy for the civil rights movement. Dr. Carey said that he had asked both Dr. King and Director Hoover not to alienate each other. He also said that he had been concerned less with the truth or falsity of any of the allegations that were made than with ending the dispute.

VII. The FBI Program Against Dr. King: 1965-1968

The public dispute between Dr. King and Director Hoover ended with their December 1, 1964, meeting. The Bureau's covert attempts to discredit Dr. King and undermine his influence in the civil rights movement did not cease, however, but continued unabated until Dr. King's death. Although the intensity of the FBI's campaign against Dr. King appears to have been reduced somewhat in 1966 and 1967, Dr. King's public stand against the war in Vietnam in mid-1967 revived the FBI's attempt to link Dr. King and the SCLC with communism.

A. Major Efforts to Discredit Dr. King: 1965-1968

1. Attempts to Discredit Dr. King With Churches

On February 1, 1965, the Domestic Intelligence Division learned that Dr. King was scheduled to speak at the Davenport, Iowa, Catholic Interracial Council's banquet and receive a "Pacem in Terris" award in memory of Pope John. Internal

Security Section chief Frederick Baumgardner observed, "It is shocking indeed that King continues to be honored by religious groups." Baumgardner recommended that Assistant Director Malone contact Francis Cardinal Spellman and suggest that "in the end it might well be embarrassing to the Catholic Church for having given honors to King." The Director noted on the memorandum, "I see no need to further approach Spellman"; he was apparently alluding to the unsuccessful attempt to sabotage Dr. King's audience with the Pope through Spellman's intervention. There is no record of any further action.

In February 1966, Dr. King held a press conference following a meeting with the Reverend John P. Cody, Archbishop of the Chicago Diocese of the Roman Catholic Church, and announced that he and Cody were in agreement on general civil rights goals and that he hoped priests and nuns in Chicago would participate in SCLC programs. The Domestic Intelligence Division subsequently recommended that a special agent acquainted with the Archbishop brief him about Dr. King to aid "the Archbishop in determining the degree of cooperation his archdiocese will extend to King's program in Chicago and [to] result in a lessening of King's influence in Chicago."

The Archbishop was briefed on February 24, 1966, "along the lines discussed with Assistant Director Sullivan." The agent who conducted the briefing wrote that he felt "certain that [Cody] will do everything possible to neutralize King's effect in this area."

In April 1966 the FBI Legal Attache in Paris requested permission to inform the pastor of the American Church in Paris of Dr. King's background "in an effort to convince him that his continued support of Martin Luther King may result in embarrassment for him and the American Church in Paris." The pastor was briefed on May 9, 1966. According to the agent who conducted the briefing, the pastor was skeptical about the FBI allegations, but promised to keep the information in mind for future dealings with Dr. King.

2. Attempts to Discredit Dr. King With Heads of Government Agencies

In March 1965 the FBI contacted former Florida Governor LeRoy Collins. Collins was then Director of the Community Relations Service, Department of Commerce, a position the Bureau viewed as "something of a 'mediator' in problems relating to the racial field." The FBI told Collins that Corretta King had criticized his participation in developments in Selma, Alabama and had said that Collins was "blinded by prejudice." A copy of the December 1964 monograph about Dr. King was also sent to Collins, "in view of [his] important position relative to the racial movement."

Also in March 1965 the FBI learned that the Internal Revenue Service intended to invite Dr. King as one of 19 guest lecturers at a series of seminars on Equal Employment Opportunities. When the IRS requested routine name checks on the 19 individuals, Director Hoover approved a Domestic Intelligence Division request to send the IRS a copy of the December 1964 monograph; normal procedures were followed in checking the other 18 people.

In December 1966 Domestic Intelligence Director William Sullivan reported that he had met with Ambassador U. Alexis Johnson during a tour of the FBI's Legal Attache Office in Japan and was surprised to learn that Johnson was unaware of allegations that communists were influencing Dr. King. Sullivan recommended that Johnson be sent a copy of the monograph about Dr. King "because of his position." Director Hoover approved the plan, and a copy of the monograph was sent to the FBI Legal Attache in Tokyo for hand-delivery to the Ambassador.

Dr. King publicly announced his opposition to American involvement in the war in Vietnam in a speech at New York's Riverside Church on April 4, 1967. Six days later, Charles Brennan of the Domestic Intelligence Division recommended the circulation of an updated draft of the King monograph to the White House. Brennan's memorandum states that the revised monograph contained allegations about communist influence over Dr. King as well as personally derogatory allegations.

Director Hoover approved and copies of the revised monograph were sent to the White House, the Secretary of State, the Secretary of Defense, the Director of the Secret Service, and the Attorney General. A copy was subsequently sent to the Commandant of the Marine Corps, who had been interested in "King's activities in the civil rights movement but recently had become quite concerned as to whether there are any subversive influences which have caused King to link the civil rights movement with the anti-Vietnam War movement." The Domestic Intelligence Division recommended that a copy be given to the Marine Commandant because "it is felt would definitely be to the benefit of [the Commandant] and to the Bureau...."

In February 1968, FBI Headquarters learned that Dr. King planned a "Washington Spring Project" for April 1968. According to a Domestic Intelligence Division memorandum, the Director suggested that the King monograph be again revised. That memorandum noted:

"Bringing this monograph up-to-date and disseminating it at high level prior to King's 'Washington Spring Project' should serve again to remind top-level officials in Government of the wholly disreputable character of King....

"Because of the importance of doing a thorough job on this, we will conduct an exhaustive field review to bring together the most complete and up-to-date information and to present it in a hard-hitting manner."

The revised monograph, dated March 12, 1968, was disseminated to the White House, the Attorney General, and the heads of various government intelligence agencies.

3. Attempts to Discredit Dr. King By Using the Press

Despite Cartha DeLoach's assurances to Andrew Young and Ralph Abernathy that the FBI would never disseminate information to the press, the Bureau continued its efforts to cultivate "friendly" news sources that would be willing to release information unfavorable to Dr. King. Ralph McGill, the pro-civil rights editor of the Atlanta *Constitution*, was a major focus of the Bureau's attentions. The Bureau apparently first furnished McGill with derogatory information about Dr. King as part of an attempt to dissuade community leaders in Atlanta from participating in a banquet planned to honor Dr. King upon his return from the Nobel Prize ceremonies. After a meeting with McGill, William Sullivan reported that McGill said that he had stopped speaking favorably of Dr. King, that he had refused to take an active part in preparing for the banquet, and that he had even taken steps to undermine the banquet. McGill's version of what transpired will never be known, since McGill is deceased. According to Sullivan's memorandum, however:

"Mr. McGill told me that following my first discussion with him a few weeks ago he contacted a banker friend in Atlanta who was helping to finance the banquet to be given King next Wednesday night. The banker was disturbed and said he would contact some other bankers also involved and see if support could be quietly withdrawn. McGill's friend and some of the bankers did take steps to withdraw but this was very quickly relayed to bankers in Haiti who were on the threshold of an important financial deal with the Atlanta, Georgia, bankers. They took the position that if the Atlanta bankers did not support the Martin Luther King party, their financial deal with these Georgia bankers was off. . . . As a result they got cold feet and decided to go ahead with financing King's party.

"McGill told me that .... a Catholic leader in Georgia, an Episcopal clergyman and a Jewish rabbi are also quite active in support of this party for King ... I told him that ... he might want to explore very confidentially and discreetly the subject matter with these three men. . . .

"McGill told me that he thinks it is too late now, especially in view of the financial interest of the Georgia bankers in the Haiti deal, to prevent the banquet from taking place. However, McGill said he would do what he could to encourage key people to limit their praise and support of King as much as possible.

"McGill also told me that he is taking steps through [a Negro leader] to get key Negro leaders to unite in opposition to King and to gradually force him out of the civil rights movement if at all possible."

The FBI subsequently told the White House that McGill: "believes that the very best thing that could happen would be to have King step completely out of the civil rights movement and public life, for he feels that if this is not done, sooner or later King will be publicly exposed. Mr. McGill believes that an exposure of King will do irreparable harm to the civil rights movement in which he, Mr. McGill, and others are so interested and have worked so hard for; and likewise it will do injury to different citizens of the country who have been supporting King."

In late May 1965, a reporter from United Press International requested the Bureau for information about Dr. King for use in a series of articles about the civil rights leader. The Special Agent in Charge in Atlanta recommended that the Bureau give the reporter both public source and confidential information about Dr. King because the reporter "is the UPI's authority in the South on the Negro movement and his articles carry a great deal of influence and [the SAC did not believe] that he would prepare anything flattering or favorable to King." The Director approved a recommendation that the reporter be supplied with a public source document and with a "short summation" of allegations concerning communist influence over Dr. King to be used "merely for orientation purposes."

In October 1966, the Domestic Intelligence Division recommended that an article "indicting King for his failure to take a stand on the [black power] issue and at the same time exposing the degree of communist influence on him" be given to a newspaper contact "friendly" to the Bureau, "such as ... [the] Editor of *U.S. News and World Report*."

"It is felt that the public should again be reminded of this communist influence on King, and the current controversy among civil rights leaders makes this timely to do so."

Attached to the memorandum was a proposed article which noted that the efforts of several civil rights leaders to denounce "Black Power" had been "undermined by one man in the civil rights movement who holds in his hands the power to silence the rabble rousers and to give the movement renewed momentum." The article attributed Dr. King's equivocation to his advisers, who were alleged to have had affiliations with the Communist Party or organizations associated with the Party. Dr. King's decision to oppose the Vietnamese war was also attributed to these advisers.

One project involving the mass media which the FBI felt had been particularly successful was its attempt to prevent Dr. King from obtaining contributions from James Hoffa of the Teamsters Union. In October 1966, the FBI discovered that Dr. King planned to meet with Hoffa, but that Dr. King had wanted to avoid publicity because, in the words of the Bureau:

"Disclosure of King's transparent attempt to blackmail Hoffa with the large Negro membership of Hoffa's union, to solve the Southern Christian Leadership Conference's financial problems, would cause an uproar among leaders of organizations having large Negro memberships, pointing out their own vulnerability to such a squeeze by any unscrupulous civil rights leader. This potential collusion between large labor unions and the civil rights movement could also react to the detriment of the Negro in that through large financial donations, an unscrupulous labor leader could subvert the legitimate aims and objectives of the civil rights movement to his own purposes."

The Crime Records Division prepared an article for public release raising the question of "who really gets squeezed when these two pythons get together." The Domestic Intelligence Division also recommended: "a Bureau official be designated now to alert friendly news media of the meeting once the meeting date is learned so that arrangements can be made for appropriate press coverage of the planned meeting to expose and disrupt it."

Director Hoover's "O.K." appears below that recommendation.

On discovering that the meeting was about to occur, the Crime Records Division notified a reporter for the New York *Daily News* and a national columnist. "News photographers and wire services are also being alerted to give coverage. . . ."

A Crime Records Division memorandum on the following day reported that "in view of publicity in the New York *Daily News* regarding this proposed meeting, King and his aides had decided that it would be unwise to meet with Hoffa." The Bureau then notified reporters that Dr. King was coming to Washington, D.C. The reporters "cornered" Dr. King as he came off the plane and quizzed him about the proposed meeting. The Crime Records Division reported these events to the Director with the assessment that "our counterintelligence aim to thwart King from receiving money from the Teamsters has been quite successful to date." Director Hoover initialed the memorandum reporting this news, "Excellent."

In March 1967 Director Hoover approved a recommendation by the Domestic Intelligence Division to furnish "friendly" reporters questions to ask Dr. King. The Intelligence Division believed that Dr. King would be particularly "vulnerable" to questions concerning his opposition to the war in Vietnam, and recommended that a reporter be selected to interview Dr. King "ostensibly to question King about his new book," but with the objective of bringing out the foreign policy aspects of Dr. King's philosophy.

This could then be linked to show that King's current policies remarkably parallel communist efforts. This would cause extreme embarrassment to King.

In October 1967 the Domestic Intelligence Division recommended that an editorial in a Negro magazine, which criticized Dr. King for his stance on the Vietnam war, be given to "friendly news sources." The purpose of the dissemination was to "publicize King as a traitor to his country and his race" and to "reduce his income" from a series of shows given by Harry Belafonte to earn funds for the SCLC. The recommendation was approved by the Director and is marked "Handled 10/28/67."

4. Attempts to Discredit Dr. King With Major Political and Financial Leaders

In March 1965 the FBI learned that a "Martin Luther King Day" was being planned in a major city. The Domestic Intelligence Division recommended that the Special Agent in. Charge "personally meet with the Governor and brief him concerning King" in order to "induce him to minimize the affair and especially the award for King."

The Domestic Intelligence Division memorandum was initialed by the Director and bears the handwritten notation, "handled 3-5-65, WCS[ullivan]."

In October 1966 the FBI learned that Dr. King had met with McGeorge Bundy, then Director of the Ford Foundation, and received a tentative offer of a grant for the SCLC. The Domestic Intelligence Division decided that officials of the Foundation might not be aware of the "subversive backgrounds of King's principal advisers," but that if they were briefed, "this might preclude any assistance being granted." Director Hoover approved a plan to have a former FBI agent, who was then a vice-president of the Ford Motor Company, approach Bundy. The ex-agent was contacted, briefed on Dr. King, and according to DeLoach, "stated he would personally contact Bundy in an effort to put a stop to King receiving any funds from the Ford Foundation."

In a memorandum dated October 26, 1966, DeLoach reported that the ex-agent had contacted Bundy, but that Bundy had refused to talk with him about Dr. King, saying that he would only talk with a person having first-hand knowledge about Dr. King, and would not listen to rumors. DeLoach recommended that the FBI not directly approach Bundy, since "it is doubtful that contact with him by the FBI will convince him one way or another." Director Hoover wrote on DeLoach's memorandum, "Yes. We would get no where with Bundy."

5. Attempts to Discredit Dr. King With Congressional Leaders

According to a memorandum by Assistant to the Director DeLoach, Speaker of the House John McCormack requested a briefing about Dr. King's background and activities in August 1965. DeLoach reported that he briefed McCormack for 45 minutes about Dr. King's private life and about possible communist influence over Dr. King. According to DeLoach, McCormack stated that "he now recognized the gravity of the situation and that something obviously must be done about it." McCormack was not interviewed by the committee staff.

Not all Congressional inquiries about Dr. King, however, were answered by the Bureau. For example, in January 1968, DeLoach reported that he had met with Senator Robert C. Byrd at the Senator's request. DeLoach's memorandum of the meeting states that the Senator expressed concern over Dr. King's plan for demonstrations in Washington, D.C. during the summer and said that it was time Dr. King "met his Waterloo." DeLoach's memorandum states that Senator Byrd asked if the FBI would prepare a speech about Dr. King which he could deliver on the floor of the Senate. DeLoach declined to provide any information that was not on the public record, although he did promise to keep the Senator informed of new public source items. The Committee staff did not interview Senator Byrd.

B. COINTELPRO Operations Against Dr. King and His Associates

The FBI elevated its activities against Dr. King and his associates to the status of formal counterintelligence programs (COINTELPRO) during this period. In July 1966, the Director instructed the New York field office that "immediate steps should be taken to discredit, expose, or otherwise neutralize Adviser A's role as a clandestine communist." An agent was assigned full-time to "carefully review the [Adviser A] case file seeking possible counterintelligence approaches." He reported that there was no derogatory information on Adviser A's personal life, and that the only "effective way to neutralize [him] is by public exposure" of his alleged Communist Party associations. None of the FBI's efforts against Adviser A appear to have met success.

The FBI considered initiating a formal COINTELPRO to discredit Dr. King and Dr. Benjamin Spock in May 1967 when rumors developed concerning the possibility that King and Spock might run as "peace" candidates in the 1968 presidential election. The New York field office recommended postponing the effort to expose "communist connections" of persons associated with King and Spock until they had formally announced their candidacy. The Chicago field office proposed waiting until the summer of 1968, reasoning that by then the Administration would have either resolved the Vietnam conflict or, if not, the Communist Party would be emphasizing the peace theme, and exposure of Communist Party links with the King-Spock campaign "would doubtlessly be appreciated by the Administration." While the Chicago field office felt that the Bureau should not "rule out" the use of "flyers, leaflets, cards and bumper stickers" to discredit the King-Spock ticket, it recommended "the use of a political columnist or reporter for this purpose." Apparently no steps were taken to implement the plan.

In August 1967 the Bureau initiated a COINTELPRO captioned "Black Nationalist-Hate Groups." This program is extensively described in the Staff Report on COINTELPRO. The document initiating the program states:

"The purpose of this new counterintelligence endeavor is to expose, disrupt, misdirect, discredit, or otherwise neutralize the activities of black-nationalist, hate-type organizations and groupings, their leadership, spokesmen, membership and supporters, and to counter their propensity for violence and civil disorder.

"Intensified attention under this program should be afforded to the activities of such groups as the Student Nonviolent Coordinating Committee, Southern Christian Leadership Conference, Revolutionary Action Movement, the Deacons for Defense and Justice, Congress of Racial Equality, and the Nation of Islam."

The Domestic Intelligence Division expanded the Black Nationalist-Hate Groups COINTELPRO in February 1968. The instructions to the field offices listed as a "goal":

"Prevent the rise of a 'messiah' who could unify and electrify the militant black nationalist movement. Malcolm X might have been such a 'messiah'; he is the martyr of the movement today. Martin Luther King, Stokely Carmichael, and Elijah Muhammed all aspire to this position. Elijah Muhammed is less of a threat because of his age. King could be a real contender for this position should he abandon his supposed 'obedience' to 'white, liberal doctrines' (nonviolence) and embrace black nationalism."

The SCLC was retained as a "primary target" of the COINTELPRO, and Martin Luther King's name was added to the list of persons who were targets.

The supervisor of the Black Nationalist COINTELPRO told the Committee that he could recall no counterintelligence activities directed against the SCLC, but that several were taken against Dr. King.

C. The FBI's Efforts to Discredit Dr. King During His Last Months

Between 1965 and early 1967, the files indicate that Bureau concern about Dr. King had decreased. This concern was revived by Dr. King's April 4, 1967, speech at New York's Riverside Church, in which he opposed the Administration's position in Vietnam. The FBI interpreted this position as proof he "has been influenced by communist advisers," and noted that King's remarks were "a direct parallel of the communist position on Vietnam." A week after the speech the FBI sent the White House and the Justice Department a revised edition of the printed King monograph.

In early December 1967 Dr. King announced plans to hold demonstrations in major American cities, including Washington, D.C., to spur Congress into enacting civil rights legislation. The FBI followed closely developments in Dr. King's "Washington Spring Project" forwarding to the White House information concerning Adviser A's fund-raising activities and Dr. King's plans to tape a lecture series for a foreign television system, allegedly to raise funds for the project.

In February 1968 the FBI again revised the King monograph and distributed it to certain officials in the Executive Branch. The Domestic Intelligence Division memorandum recommending the new monograph stated that its dissemination "prior to King's 'Washington Spring Project' should serve again to remind top-level officials in Government of the wholly disreputable character of King."

In early March, the Bureau broadened its Black Nationalist-Hate Groups COINTELPRO explicitly to include Dr. King. Toward the end of the month, the FBI began to disseminate information to the press "designed to curtail success of Martin Luther King's fund raising campaign for the Washington Spring Project." The first of many plans included circulating a story "that King does not need contributions from the 70,000 people he solicited. Since the churches have offered support, no more money is needed and any contributed would only be used by King for other purposes. This item would need nation-wide circulation in order to reach all the potential contributors and curtail their donations."

On March 25, the Bureau approved a plan to mail an anonymous letter to a civil rights leader in Selma, Alabama, who was "miffed" with Dr. King, and a copy of that letter to a Selma newspaper, hoping that the newspaper might interview the leader about its contents. The Bureau described the purpose of the letter as calling "to the attention of [the civil rights leader] that King is merely using the Negroes of the Selma area for his own personal aggrandizement; that he is not genuinely interested in their welfare, but only in their donations; that in all probability the individuals going to Washington for the Spring Project will be left stranded without suitable housing or food. The letter should also play up the possibility of violence."

There is no indication in FBI files that the letter was mailed.

During the latter part of March, Dr. King went to Memphis, Tennessee, where a strike by Sanitation Workers had erupted into violent riots.

A March 28, 1968, Domestic Intelligence Division memorandum stated:

"A sanitation strike has been going on in Memphis for some time. Martin Luther King, Jr., today led a march composed of 5,000 to 6,000 people through the streets of Memphis. King was in an automobile preceding the marchers. As the march developed, acts of violence and vandalism broke out including the breaking of windows in stores and some looting.

"This clearly demonstrates that acts of so-called nonviolence advocated by King cannot be controlled. The same thing could happen in his planned massive civil disobedience for Washington in April.

"Attached is a blind memorandum pointing out the above, which if you approve, should be made available by Crime Records Division to cooperative news media sources."

The memorandum carried Director Hoover's "O.K." and the notation, "handled on 3/28/68."

On March 29,1968, the Domestic Intelligence Division recommended that the following article be furnished to a cooperative news source:

"Martin Luther King, during the sanitation workers' strike in Memphis, Tennessee, has urged Negroes to boycott downtown white merchants to achieve Negro demands. On 3/29/68 King led a march for the sanitation workers. Like Judas leading lambs to slaughter King led the marchers to violence, and when the violence broke out, King disappeared.

"The fine Hotel Lorraine in Memphis is owned and patronized exclusively by Negroes but King didn't go there for his hasty exit. Instead King decided the plush Holiday Inn Motel, white owned, operated and almost exclusively patronized, was the place to 'cool it.' There will be no boycott of white merchants for King, only for his followers."

On April 4, Dr. King returned to Memphis. This time he registered at the Lorraine Hotel. We have discovered no evidence that the FBI was responsible for Dr. King's move to the Lorraine Hotel.

D. Attempts to Discredit Dr. King's Reputation After His Death

The FBI's attempts to discredit Dr. King did not end with his death. In March 1969 the Bureau was informed that Congress was considering declaring Dr. King's birthday a national holiday, and that members of the House Committee on Internal Security might be contacting the Bureau for a briefing about Dr.

King. The Crime Records Division recommended briefing the Congressmen because they were "in a position to keep the bill from being reported out of Committee" if "they realize King was a scoundrel." DeLoach noted: "This is a delicate matter — but can be handled very cautiously." Director Hoover wrote, "I agree. It must be handled very cautiously."

In April 1969 FBI Headquarters received a recommendation for a counterintelligence program from the Atlanta Field Office. The nature of the proposed program has not been revealed to the Committee. A memorandum concerning the plan which the Bureau has given to the Committee, however, notes that the plan might be used "in the event the Bureau is inclined to entertain counterintelligence action against Coretta Scott King and/or the continuous projection of the public image of Martin Luther King ...." The Director informed the Atlanta office that "the Bureau does not desire counterintelligence action against Coretta King of the nature you suggest at this time."

Conclusion

Although it is impossible to gauge the full extent to which the FBI's discrediting programs affected the civil rights movement, the fact that there was impact is unquestionable.

Rumors circulated by the FBI had a profound impact on the SCLC's ability to raise funds. According to Congressman Andrew Young, a personal friend and associate of Dr. King, the FBI's effort against Dr. King and the SCLC "chilled contributions. There were direct attempts at some of our larger contributors who told us that they had been told by agents that Martin had a Swiss bank account, or that Martin had confiscated some of the monies from the March on Washington for his personal use. None of that was true." Harry Wachtel, one of Dr. King's legal counsels who handled many of the financial and fund raising activities of the SCLC, emphasized that the SCLC was always in need of funds. "Getting a grant or getting a contribution is a very fragile thing. A grant delayed has a very serious impact on an organization whose financial condition was pretty rough." Wachtel testified that the SCLC continually had to overcome rumors of poor financial management and communist connections:

"The material ... stayed in the political bloodstream all the way through to the time of Dr. King's death, and even after. In our efforts to build a King Center, it was around. It was like a contamination."

The SCLC leadership assumed that anything said in meetings or over the telephone would be intercepted by wiretaps, bugs, or informants. Ironically, the FBI memorandum reporting that a wiretap of the SCLC's Atlanta office was feasible stated:

"In the past when interviews have been conducted in the office of Southern Christian Leadership Conference certain employees when asked a question, in a half joking manner and a half serious manner replied, 'You should know that already, don't you have our wires tapped?' It is noted in the past the State of Georgia has conducted investigations regarding subject and Southern Christian Leadership Conference."

Harry Wachtel commented on the impact constant surveillance on members of the SCLC:

"When you live in a fishbowl, you act like you're in a fishbowl, whether you do it consciously or unconsciously.... I can't put specifics before you, except to say that it beggars the imagination not to believe that the SCLC, Dr. King, and all its leaders were not chilled or inhibited from all kinds of activities, political and even social."

Wachtel also pointed out the ramifications stemming from the Government's advance knowledge of what civil rights leaders were thinking:

"It is like political intelligence. It did not chill us from saying it, but it affected the strategies and tactics because the people you were having strategies and tactics about were privy to what you were about. They knew your doubts. . . . Take events like strategies in Atlantic City.... Decision-making concerning which way to go, joining one challenge or not, supporting a particular situation or not, had to be limited very strongly by the fact that information which was expressed by telephone, or which could even possibly be picked up by bugging, would be in the hands of the President."

Perhaps most difficult to gauge is the personal impact of the Bureau's programs. Congressman Young told the Committee that while Dr. King was not deterred by the attacks which are now known to have been instigated in part by the FBI, there is "no question" but that he was personally affected:

"It was a great burden to be attacked by people he respected, particularly when the attacks engendered by the FBI came from people like Ralph McGill. He sat down and cried at the New York *Times* editorial about his statement on Vietnam, but this just made him more determined. It was a great personal suffering, but since we don't really know all that they did, we have no way of knowing the ways that they affected us."